THE BIG BOOK OF CHRISTMAS

THE BIG BOOK OF CHRISTMAS

Poems, plays, carols
and things to make and do

Chosen by
GABY MORGAN

MACMILLAN CHILDREN'S BOOKS

For the staff and pupils at Shottermill Infant School, Haslemere, and Happy Christmas to the Morgan, Weston, Dornan, Andjel-Davies, Shemmans and Harries families and Molly Dallas and John Crosse.

First published 2005
by Macmillan Children's Books
a division of Macmillan Publishers Limited
20 New Wharf Road, London N1 9RR
Basingstoke and Oxford
www.panmacmillan.com

Associated companies throughout the world

ISBN 0 330 43647 3

1 3 5 7 9 8 6 4 2

A CIP catalogue record for this book is available from the British Library.

Printed by Mackays of Chatham plc, Chatham, Kent.

Contents

Contents

Contents

Contents

Christmas Carols and Songs

Plays for Christmas

Contents

Christmas Greetings!

For me, Christmas morning is still one of the most exciting times of the year. I'm feeling all tingly right now, just at the thought of it. As a child, I was bursting with excitement when I woke up on Christmas morning and looked to see what Father Christmas had left me in the stocking at the foot of my bed. (In those days, most people in Britain used to call him Father Christmas. Nowadays, the name Santa Claus seems to be more popular but, whatever we call him, we all know who we mean.) Now that I have a son of my own, I'm excited to see what's in *his* Christmas stocking, but I love all the other Christmas traditions too, down to the special cooking smells that slowly spread around the house as the day goes on.

There are so many things to do at Christmas that we don't necessarily stop to think about why we do them, we simply see them as a part of Christmas: we bring trees into our homes and decorate them; we put up all sorts of decorations, often including holly and ivy; we eat mince pies and Christmas pudding; and we even kiss under the mistletoe. But why, why, *why*?

Take Father Christmas, for instance. How did he get the name 'Santa Claus'? Well, it actually means Saint Nicholas, who, before he became a saint or even started delivering presents every Christmas, was a bishop in ancient Turkey. He used to leave poor people gifts where they would discover them by accident: often in shoes or stockings, so people would find the gifts when they pulled them on. (This also explains why we hang stockings today.)

And what about Christmas trees? In winter, most trees have leafless branches and look dead. Fir trees, however, have bright green needles and look full of life. By bringing them into the house, we bring in new life. By adding tinsel and baubles we're adding blossom and fruit. This tradition probably dates back to the early 1600s, and it really caught on in Britain in the 1840s when Queen Victoria's husband, Prince Albert, made Christmas trees the very latest fashion.

We bring holly and ivy into the house for a similar reason. They're also evergreen (which means that they still have leaves on, come winter-time) and they brighten up the house with living greenery. (Holly's prickly leaves are said to represent Christ's crown of thorns and the bright red berries His drops of blood.)

But what about mistletoe? Today, the tradition is that you get to kiss anyone who's standing under the mistletoe, whether they're there by accident or if you deliberately steered them under it! The tradition dates back to long before Christianity reached Britain. According to Norse myth, Balder the god of light was killed by an arrow made from mistletoe, so his mother, the goddess Frigga, snatched it up from the ground and planted it in a tree, out of harm's way. That's why we still hang up mistletoe today.

Over time, it was thought to have healing properties and then it became a good-luck charm . . . then it was thought to bring a happy marriage and plenty of children. So now you can see where the kissing part came in.

Which brings me to family and friends, and so to

Christmas cards and Christmas presents. It's hard to imagine Christmas without either but, in Britain, New Year's Day used to be a much more important celebration than Christmas Day. December 25th used to be the date of a big festival, back in Roman times (thousands of years ago), celebrating the birth of the sun in the sky. Presents were given then but, when Christians chose the date to celebrate Christ's birthday – no one was saying that Jesus was actually born on this date; it's simply a day put aside to celebrate – presents weren't a part of it. Like so many of our traditions, the idea of present-giving came over from Germany, in the 1840s. By the 1870s it was common practice.

As for cards, there were sheets of paper with Christmas scenes printed on them as long ago as the fifteenth century – that's over five hundred years ago – but they usually contained New Year's greetings. Proper printed Christmas cards first appeared in England in 1843. It was the idea of a man named Henry Cole, and they came along at just the right time. Not only had the Penny Post recently been introduced, but also envelopes had just been invented . . . and you need envelopes to put the cards in! Christmas cards were an instant hit, and the idea spread across the world.

For me, the countdown to Christmas wouldn't be complete without an advent calendar. ('Advent' simply means the period in December leading up to Christmas, by the way.) I always love seeing what's behind the little door, and knowing that, the more doors that have been opened, the nearer it is to Christmas Day itself. (The very first advent calendars were made in Germany at the end of the nineteenth century. They were very large and had a chocolate behind every door.)

While we're on the subject of food, what about mince pies and Christmas pudding? Mince pies really did use to have minced meat in them, along with the fruit and spices. They also used to be a different shape. They were cooked to look like Christ's crib and, by the 1600s, people were even baking little pastry baby Jesuses to go on top of them!

Christmas pudding has been through even more dramatic changes. It started life as a kind of porridge. The idea was that you ate it *before* Christmas Day so that you'd leave plenty of room for all those Christmas goodies. Then, by the 1590s, it was eaten on the day itself and was much more solid (because it was packed full of extra ingredients). Then it was banned in England by Oliver Cromwell's Puritans, along with most of the other fun parts of Christmas . . . only to make a dramatic return to the Christmas dinner table in 1714, when King George I was on the throne. In fact, he loved his puds so much that he was nicknamed the 'pudding king'.

And what about Christmas crackers, with their 'bangs', jokes and novelties? Although there's still some disagreement as to when the idea was first dreamed up, there's no denying that it was a man called Tom Smith who put all these different elements together. Tom used to sell sweets, and he often put little mottoes inside the wrappers with them. He then decided to wrap little novelties and toys with the mottoes . . . and to make the wrapping more exciting by having it pull apart. Then came the 'bang' (legend has it that he got the idea from sparks popping in his fireplace). In 1846, the cracker as we know it was born.

These are just some of the traditions that survive to this day and go together to make Christmas such a magical and special time of year. Others include carol-singing and pantomimes, and you can probably think of some of your own. While I'm on the subject of thinking, can you remember the names of Father Christmas's flying reindeer – apart from Rudolph, that is? *Everyone* remembers Rudolph. I'll give you a clue: there are eight of them. You'll find the answer at the bottom of this page.)

I think you'll agree that this wonderful book has really captured the magic of Christmas. In it you'll find a whole host of poems: funny ones, sad ones, poems which bring a tear to your eyes or joy to your heart. What they all do is make you feel Christmassy! Then there are the mouth-watering Christmas recipes, the Christmas things to make and do, along with some specially written plays and a simple retelling of the Christmas story itself.

I love this book and I will be bringing it out with my Christmas decorations every year. I've no doubt, reading it with my family will quickly become a part of the Christmas ritual in my home. Which leaves me with one last, very important, thing to say: Merry Christmas, everyone!

Philip Ardagh, 2005

Answers:
The flying reindeer are: Dasher, Dancer, Prancer, Vixen, Comet, Cupid, Donner (though he's sometimes called Donder) and Blitzen

The Christmas Story

God's people in Israel were very alone and afraid. They had many enemies and were in grave danger. They lived under foreign rule, and felt powerless. They needed God's help, but they thought that God had forgotten them.

'Where is God?' they asked. 'Doesn't He care about us any more?'

God sent a man called Isaiah to comfort the people. Isaiah was a prophet – he could tell the people what God wanted to say.

'Don't worry,' said Isaiah. 'God hasn't forgotten you. He loves all His people. And to show you how much He loves you, He is going to send you a special child to lead you out of danger. This child will be a mighty king, and he will save you from all your enemies. When he comes, you will live in peace once more.'

God also sent a prophet called Micah, who told the people a surprising thing. He said that God's new king was going to come from a place called Bethlehem. This astonished the people, as Bethlehem was such a tiny, unimportant town. They couldn't believe it.

The people of Israel waited a long time for their king to come. They were excited about Isaiah's promise and were impatient to meet the king. They remembered great King David who had fought so valiantly for them long ago, and they hoped that their new king would be just like David and save them from their enemies.

Many years later, in Nazareth, a small town in the north of Israel, a young woman called Mary was busy tidying her house. She was happy because she was going to marry a kind man called Joseph. Joseph was a carpenter. He was also a descendant of the great King David, so he came from an important Jewish family.

Mary was working away quietly when suddenly an angel appeared from nowhere. Mary was terrified.

The angel told her: 'Don't be afraid. I've come to bring you great news. God has chosen you to be the mother of His son, His promised king. You will call him Jesus.'

'B-but I don't understand,' Mary stuttered.

'Don't worry,' said the angel gently. 'Anything is possible for God. He will take care of you.'

Mary bowed low and murmured, 'I am very honoured. I will be happy to do what God wants me to.'

And with that, the angel left her.

The time came for Mary to give birth to her son. She wanted to have the baby at home, surrounded by her family, but this was not to be. Far away in Rome, the Emperor Augustus had made a decision that changed everything for Mary and Joseph. Augustus had decided that he needed more money for his empire, so he told everyone to go back to the town where they were born.

'I need to know how many people there are in *all* the countries that I rule,' he bellowed. 'Tell them to come to their home towns and write down their names. Then I will know how much money I can get from them all.'

So, instead of resting at home and waiting for her baby to be born, poor, tired Mary had to climb on to a donkey and travel across the dusty, dirty desert for days and days to get to Joseph's home town, Bethlehem.

One dark evening, after many long, hard days and nights of travelling, Mary and Joseph arrived in Bethlehem. Joseph was worried about Mary. The baby was due any day now, and Mary was very tired. Joseph went straight away to an inn to find a room for the night. He knocked on the door.

'Hello, we've come all the way from Nazareth at the orders of the Emperor. We need a room for the night—'

'Sorry, mate,' said the innkeeper, not sounding at all as if he meant it, 'no rooms left. Everywhere's full. You're too late.'

'But my wife's about to have a child, and we've been travelling for days, and—' Joseph protested.

'Not my problem, is it?' said the innkeeper grumpily.

Mary looked as if she was going to cry.

'All right, all right,' the innkeeper said hastily. 'There's always the stable. Bit smelly, but at least it's warm.'

Joseph helped Mary down from the donkey and led her into the stable. He made her as comfortable as he could with blankets and straw, and helped her when the time came to give birth.

Meanwhile, out in the hills, there were some shepherds keeping watch over their sheep. They sat out every night to make sure wolves didn't come and take the sheep away. They were chatting, laughing and singing as usual when suddenly the sky blazed with light. The shepherds fell to the ground, quaking with fear. An angel had appeared in the sky.

The shepherds were speechless. They had never seen such a sight.

Then the angel said, 'Don't be afraid. I've come to bring you great news. Go to Bethlehem, the city of King David. The king that God promised you, the Saviour, Christ the Lord, has been born! This is the sign you should look for: you will find a baby wrapped in strips of cloth, and lying in a manger.'

Then suddenly the angel was joined by a multitude of angels, who filled the night air with glorious music: 'Glory to God in the highest!' they sang. 'And on earth peace to all men!'

Then the angels vanished as quickly as they had appeared.

The shepherds knew that they must do as they had been told, and hurried down to Bethlehem at once.

So Micah had been right: Jesus, the son of God, was born in Bethlehem. But was a stable the right place for the King of Israel to be born? The shepherds were in no doubt that they had found their king when they arrived at the stable. There was Jesus, wrapped in strips of cloth and lying in the manger, just as the angel had told them. But he wasn't surrounded by servants and riches as a king should be – only an ox and a donkey looked on as Mary sang softly to her baby son.

While the shepherds were worshipping the Christ child, a bright new star appeared in the heavens. It caught the attention of three wise men from the east. They recognized the star as a long–awaited sign that a new king had been born, so straight away they set off to find him.

The wise men stopped in Jerusalem and went to see King Herod.

'We've come to see the newborn king,' they announced.

'I am the only king around here,' Herod answered angrily.

Then he thought of a plan. If these wise men could tell him where the new king was, Herod could have him killed, and then his throne would be safe.

'Are you talking of God's promised king?' he asked the wise men, smiling as he spoke. 'The prophets told our people that such a child would be born in Bethlehem. You must go there now – if you find the boy, come and tell me so that I can worship him, too.'

The wise men did not know that Herod planned to kill Jesus, so they agreed to go to Bethlehem.

They followed the bright star until it stopped over the place where Jesus lay, and they found Mary and Joseph, and the baby lying in the manger. They presented precious gifts to the child.

'I bring gold,' said the first king.

'I bring frankincense,' said the second.

'I bring myrrh,' said the third.

Mary watched in astonishment as these wise men in their fine, rich robes offered their strange, costly gifts and then bowed down and worshipped her tiny son. She would never forget this day for as long as she lived.

Anna Wilson

Christmas Poems

A Christmas Blessing

God bless the master of this house,
    The mistress also,
And all the little children
    That round the table go;
And all your kin and kinsfolk,
    That dwell both far and near;
I wish you a Merry Christmas
    And a Happy New Year.

Anon.

Just Doing My Job

I'm one of Herod's Henchmen.
We don't have much to say,
We just charge through the audience
In a Henchman sort of way.

We all wear woolly helmets
To hide our hair and ears,
And wellingtons sprayed silver
To match our tinfoil spears.

Our swords are made of cardboard
So blood will not be spilled
If we trip and stab a parent
When the hall's completely filled.

We don't look VERY scary,
We're mostly small and shy,
And some of us wear glasses,
But we give the thing a try.

We whisper Henchman noises
While Herod hunts for strangers,
And then we all charge out again
Like nervous Power Rangers.

Yet when the play is over
And Miss is out of breath
We'll charge like Henchmen through the hall
And scare our Mums to death.

Clare Bevan

Infant Nativity Play

Mary in a pale blue cloak,
Joseph with a towel over his head,
Held in place by an elastic belt with snake clasp,
Approached the cardboard Inn
And knocked.

'Have you a room?' asked Joseph.
'Sorry,' said the Innkeeper, shaking his little head.
'But we have travelled far,' said Joseph.
'No room at the Inn.'
'And we are tired, very tired.'
'We are all full up and have no room.'
'And my dear wife is to have a baby.'
'We have no room at the Inn,' said the Innkeeper.
'Oh please,' begged Joseph, 'just for the night.'

The Innkeeper,
In a pale brown dressing gown
And bright red slippers,
Observed the little travellers
Sad and weary and far from home
And scratched his head.
'Have my room,' he said, smiling,
'And I'll sleep in the stable.'

Gervase Phinn

Nativity Play Plan

Church
Leader: Sistas and broddas and everybody,
same like we did sey –
we a-go keepup Jesus birtday.

Members: Yes! Yes!
We a-go keepup Jesus birtday.

Church
Leader: Mista Daaswell, bring yu donkey
Mas Pinnty, yu bring yu pony.
All will behave good-good with clappin
    and praisin.

Mista Slim, yu bring two sheep
wha will neither move nor sleep.
Faada B— two bright wing fowl
wha will look like them nevva bawl.

Sistas and broddas and everybody,
we a-go keepup Jesus birtday.
We sey we a-go do that.
A wha we sey we a-go do?

Members: We a-go keepup Jesus birtday.
Yes! Yes!
We a-go keepup Jesus birtday.

Church Leader:	Cousin Sue, bring yu big sow.
	Aunt Cita, bring yu red cow.
	All will behave good-good with singin and dancin.

Beagle and Man-Tom and Big Ben,
yu come turn in-a Wise Men.
Modda M will bring her new-new child
to be the new Jesus child.

Sistas and broddas and everybody,
we a-go keepup Jesus birtday.
We sey we a-go do that.
A wha we sey we a-go do?

Members:	We a-go keepup Jesus birtday.
	Yes! Yes!
	We a-go keepup Jesus birtday . . .

James Berry

Nativity

I wrapped a toilet roll with paper
And drew a King on it
Complete with crown and a gift for the child.

Then I made another,
With a turban because he was from the east
Which I knew was romantic and far away,
Without any clear idea where.

And yet another, Mrs Harman said there were three,
With gifts of Gold, Frankenstein and Mire,
Or so I thought.

Then shepherds, more toilet rolls,
and cotton wool for sheep.

An angel was a toilet roll with wings,
Joseph was another toilet roll with a pipe-cleaner staff,
And Mary a toilet roll with a scrap of blue cloth.

The child was a blob of Plasticine
Safe in a tiny cardboard match-box manger
filled with straw.

I took it home and Mum put it on the mantelpiece
But she hid the child.
And on Christmas morning,
4 a.m. on Christmas morning,
with a cup of tea in her hand
and a bleary leave me alone I'm still asleep look in her eye,
she set me and my brother searching for the child.

Cold, cold, cold, warmer, cold, cold until hot
And we found him safely wrapped in a tissue
Inside the cupboard under the stairs.
Gently we laid him in place before his mother
A scribbled, toilet roll Virgin and that was the best Christmas.

Eric Petrie

The Sky Exploded

Night turned inside out
And suddenly was all ablaze
Across the blue-black sky
Like diamonds. It was day,
Like rainbows sparkling in salt spray,
Or waterfalls of light . . .
Not any sort of night
That anyone had ever seen before
      – or since.
The shepherds on the hill
screwed up their eyes against it
      – so bright it made them wince.
They heard the singing,
felt the wind of wild wings beating,
      – white and gleaming thunder
high in God's heaven.

All this.
All this fanfare-fuss, this mad amazing energy,
On this high hilltop,
This was not the main event.
That happened quietly behind the pub
In a shed they kept the donkey in.
There God was born
Not in a palace to be claimed by kings
Not in a rich man's house awash with *things*.
Not even underneath the angels' shining wings
But in a shed. With stuff.
For us. For ordinary us.

Jan Dean

The Singers of Bethlehem

The father sang of journeys,
The donkey sang of sleep,
The shepherd sang of fearful dreams,
Of lambswool warm and deep.

The pigeon sang of darkness,
The fieldmouse sang of light,
The oxen sang of comfort
In the hollows of the night.

The tomcat sang of strangers,
The women sang of birth,
The angels sang of miracles,
Of joy for all the Earth.

The wise men sang of wonders
That gleamed amongst the straw,
But Mary sang of one dear child
To love for evermore.

Clare Bevan

Haiku

avalanche of love
awakening of angels
a Baby is born

Celia Warren

Angels

Earth and sky,
sky and earth,
both embrace
the holy birth.

Picture angels
in that sky.
Imagine angels
there, on high.

Angel music
fills the night.
Angels wrapped
in angel light.

Candles lit
on angel chimes.
Christmas Eve.
Christmas times.

Ann Bonner

Angels

We are made from light.
Called into being we burn
Brighter than the silver white
Of hot magnesium.
More sudden than yellow phosphorus.
We are the fire of heaven;
Blue flames and golden ether.

We are from stars.
Spinning beyond the farthest galaxy
In an instant gathered to this point
We shine, speak our messages and go,
Back to the brilliance.
We are not separate, not individual.
We are what we are made of. Only
Shaped sometimes into tall-winged warriors,
Our faces solemn as swords,
Our voices joy.

The skies are cold;
Suns do not warm us;
Fire does not burn itself.
Only once we touched you
And felt a human heat.
Once, in the brightness of the frost,
Above the hills, in glittering starlight,
Once, we sang.

Jan Dean

The Innkeeper's Story

I saw a baby in a manger.

I saw a baby in a manger
With two parents, Mary and Joseph.

I saw a baby in a manger
With two parents, Mary and Joseph,
And three wise kings
Who came on four camels.
(There was one to carry the presents.)

I saw a baby in a manger
With two parents, Mary and Joseph,
And three wise kings
With their four camels,
And five shepherds,
All dusty from the hills –
Oh yes, and they had six sheep with them.
(They couldn't leave them behind because of the wolves.)

I saw a baby in a manger
With two parents, Mary and Joseph,
And three wise kings
With their four camels,
And five shepherds,
With their six sheep
That couldn't be left behind,
And seven donkeys,
And eight cows . . .
Then there were the angels.

They kept flying around singing,
And it was hard to count them,
But there must have been at least nine.

Nine angels,
Eight cows,
Seven donkeys,
Six sheep,
Five shepherds,
Four camels,
Three wise kings,
Two parents,
A baby,

And one
Very special star.

David Orme

In the Stable

I smelt the perfume borne by a king,
I felt the brush of an angel's wing,
I saw contentment when Mary smiled,
I heard the cry of her newborn child,
I tasted tears with the tip of my tongue
At the weight of the world on one so young.

Sue Cowling

Coronation

Bring him a garland of bright winter jasmine,
Twine a gold chaplet to circle his head,
Weave his crown softly now,
No thorn to harm his brow,
Wind it with kisses and small stars instead.

Sue Cowling

Manger

The servant girl brought water,
a lantern and some bread,
sweet hay for the infant,
a pillow for his head.
The pot boy welcomed strangers,
served them winter ale.
The inn man carved an angel
and hung it on a nail.

Peter Dixon

The Rocking Carol

Little Jesus, sweetly sleep, do not stir;
We will lend a coat of fur,
   We will rock you, rock you, rock you,
   We will rock you, rock you, rock you:
See the fur to keep you warm
Snugly round your tiny form.

Mary's little baby, sleep, sweetly sleep,
Sleep in comfort, slumber deep,
   We will rock you, rock you, rock you,
   We will rock you, rock you, rock you:
We will serve you all we can,
Darling, darling little man.

Percy Dearmer

Nativity

When God decided to be bones and skin and blood like us
He didn't choose a palace, nothing grand – no frills and fuss.
He slipped in through the back door, with the straw and hay
  and dust.
He just became a baby with no choice but to trust.
And love us without question, as every baby must.

But Creation knew the wonder of this tiny newborn king.
The crystal depths of space were touched, the air itself would
  sing.
The Word is flesh. The silence of the glittering stars is
  shattered. Heaven rings.
The sky blazed wild with angels, whose song was fire and
  snow.
When God lay in his mother's arms two thousand years ago.

Jan Dean

What Will They Give You?

What will they give you,
my darling baby boy –
so early this dark morning?

> Will they give you seven candles
> to guide you through the night?

> Will they give you loaves and fishes
> and water sweet as wine?

> Will they give you a boat
> that can ride through the storm?

What will they give you,
my darling baby boy –
so early this dark morning?

> Will they give you a purse
> filled with silver gleaming bright?

> Will they give you a tree
> dressed in berries cold and white?

> Will they give you a kiss
> in a garden before dawn?

What will they give you,
my darling baby boy?

Will they give you
a crown of thorns?

David Greygoose

What the Donkey Saw

No room in the inn, of course,
And not that much in the stable,
What with the shepherds, Magi, Mary,
Joseph, the heavenly host –
Not to mention the baby
Using our manger as a cot.
You couldn't have squeezed another cherub in
For love or money.

Still, in spite of the overcrowding,
I did my best to make them feel wanted.
I could see the baby and I
Would be going places together.

U. A. Fanthorpe

Little Donkey

Little donkey, what did you do,
what did you do on Christmas Eve?
'I carried a woman, her head bowed down.
I carried her into Bethlehem town.'

Little donkey, what did you hear,
what did you hear on Christmas Night?
'I heard the angels, the sky was torn
as they sang out joyfully, "Christ is born."'

Little donkey, who were you with,
who were you with on Christmas Night?
'I was with the ox who stood quite still
as the shepherds ran from the star bright hills.'

Little donkey, what did you see,
what did you see on Christmas Day?
'I saw a Babe in a manger bed,
a heavenly light about His head.'

Little donkey, who followed the Star,
who followed the Star on Christmas Night?
'Three kings of splendour and of pride
who fell to their knees at the Baby's side.'

Little donkey, what do you bear,
what do you bear to remember Him?
'I bear the Cross, the Cross on my back,
etched in velvety brown and black.
I bear the Cross to remember Him.'

Marian Swinger

Forgotten Attendants

Did a spider in that stable
spinning silken thread
begin to weave a halo
above the baby's head?

What about those beetles
scuttling round in straw
who sensed that this intruder
was one they could adore?

Was there a caterpillar
gripping the manger's rim
who stopped when level with His eyes
to bow and worship Him?

Probably some working ants
changed their routine plan
and marched in pairs to kneel before
this newborn little man.

We know the donkey, lambs and sheep
were drawn into His light
but insects would have been there too
to celebrate that night.

Peggy Poole

Wanted

WANTED a reliable STAR
to lead a small party westwards.
Bright with good sense of
direction. No timewasters.
Send CV to CHILDTREK, EARTH.

Sue Cowling

'West,' Said the Star

'West,' said the star
So West we all went,
My two friends and I,
The camels, the tent,
The gifts for the King
And food for the way.
We never expected
A babe in the hay.

Sue Cowling

Shine
(A Tanka)

Shine, bright silver star!
Lead those wise men on their way,
   Bearing richest gifts
For this child who's born today,
Laid in humble straw and hay.

John Kitching

Speeches of Kings and Shepherds

Three kings we be,
And from afar,
And through the shivering cold,
We have travelled
On horse and camel,
Guided by a star;
And we have brought the baby
Presents three,
Incense and myrrh and gold.
And here in this rough place
We kneel, to look upon his face,
And give our presents, one two three.

Shepherds are we
And from the field
Where, by our simple fire
We sat
Chatting of this and that,
Sent by an angel choir
We have come here on foot
To greet the child
With gifts – a fleece, a flute,
Warmth for the babe and music sweet;
And now we lay them at his feet.
Look! The baby smiled.

Gerard Benson

The Christmas Travellers

The frost was hard,
  the snowdrifts deep
    when shepherds left
      their flock of sheep
        and glimpsed the child
       asleep, asleep.

A new star shone
  on three Wise Men.
    each wore a cloak
     and diadem.
      From far they came
     to Bethlehem.

Wes Magee

Reminder

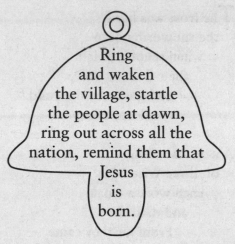

Ring
and waken
the village, startle
the people at dawn,
ring out across all the
nation, remind them that
Jesus
is
born.

Daphne Kitching

The Old Ways

The old ways live
in pale mistletoe,
in robin redbreast
and the yule log's glow,
in holly and in ivy,
wreaths of evergreen.
In these the old ways
are still seen.
In dark midwinter
when short days grow cold,
the sun fades, dwindles
sinking, as of old
then is reborn, in splendour
with the dawn
and lends its story
to the Christ Child, born
to rise in glory
and to spread His rays
down all the centuries,
through all our days.

Marian Swinger

Winter Song

Silver white
Is the world tonight
As we follow the star
That burns so bright.

Golden light
Points the way
To a child who sleeps
On a bed of hay.

Jewelled bright
On the stable floor
Are the gifts we leave
On the shining straw.

Icy white
Is the sifting snow
That covers our tracks
As we homeward go.

Cynthia Rider

Christmas Glow

My house smells of Christmas:
pine resin, cinnamon,
gingerbread, cloves.

We've made mince pies
and fir-cone swags,
pomanders and mistletoe balls.
On the wall there's a spiced apple garland.
The fir tree greens the hall.
Red-berried holly and ivy tumble
over the open front door.

My house smells of Christmas:
pine resin, cinnamon,
gingerbread, cloves:

ready for the Star
and feathers of snow,
a newborn child,
myrrh, frankincense, gold:
to light my house
with that special, Christmas glow.

Joan Poulson

Christmas

Carol-singing in the frosty air,
Holly wreaths all down the stair,
Reindeer galloping across the night,
Ivy looped with tinsel bright,
Stockings hung on ends of beds,
Trees dressed up in golds and reds,
Mince pies ready, spicy and hot,
A baby in a manger cot,
Stars to guide kings all the way . . .
. . . And we wake up to Christmas Day!

Moira Andrew

Kissing in the Snow

High in our twisted old apple tree
Grows a great clump of mistletoe
And beneath it we all stood looking up –
That Christmas out in the snow.

'We must get some down for the party.
Fetch the ladder,' urged all the girls.
No good. So it swayed there just out of reach
With its berries gleaming like pearls.

'There must be a way. *There must be!*'
There was: it was found by me.
So when there was Christmas kissing to do
In the snow we kissed under the tree.

Eric Finney

Love Is Blind

Under the mistletoe
My very short-sighted sister
and her extremely short-sighted boyfriend
take off their glasses
to kiss . . .

and miss.

Bernard Young

Three Christmas Riddles

1. Milk-white, mischievous
    cluster of pearl,
    we hang on your door-frame
    or wait in the hall.

    Don't try to avoid us
    by ducking or rushing
    but join in the fun
    of kissing and blushing.

2. Big round belly,
    cheeks aglow,
    scarlet coat –
    watch out below! –
    Touch-down, landing
    on the snow,
    with my heavy sack
    and a Ho! Ho! Ho!

3. I am the promise
    that will not break,
    I am the giving
    for you to take,

    I am the love
    and the hope and the law,
    I am the challenge
    that lies in the straw,

    I am the guest
    who has come to stay,
    I am the first-born
    of Christmas Day.

John Mole

[Answers: 1. Mistletoe 2. Santa Claus 3. The Christ Child]

Kennings – Christmas

Christmas – Cracker
Stocking – Stacker
Carol – Singer
Bell – Ringer
Good – Willer
Stomach – Filler
Money – Spender
Friendship – Mender
Party – Goer
Mind – Blower
Gift – Shopper
Cork – Popper
Table – Coaster
Drink – Toaster
Present – Bearer
Wrapping – Tearer
Sherry – Drinker
Light – Twinkler
Knitted – Sweater
Mince pie – Eater

Yasmin Hussain

Wrappings

Bubble-wrap, brown paper,
Sellotape and string,
Presents wrapped for posting,
When happy Christmassing.

Multi-coloured Santas,
Stars of red and gold,
Presents wrapped in brightness
For children, young and old.

Special bags and boxes,
Stockings tied to trees,
Presents wrapped with thoughtfulness,
Presents wrapped to please.

Not in shiny paper
With curled ribbon bows,
The first Christmas gift came
Simply wrapped, in swaddling clothes.

Daphne Kitching

Our Christmas Decorations

In our living room
flocks of paper chains fly in formation
high above our heads.

Their rustling feathers in multicoloured strands waft, light as
parrot the slightest breeze.

Tucked in the top of the picture-frame
are twigs of freshly cut holly
buttoned with deep red

berries among glossy leaves of waxy dark
green with fierce little spines.

And here's our pine-scented Christmas tree,
richly draped in necklaces
of prickly, shivering tinsel.
From the branch tips dangle blue and purple globes,
glowing planets in a glittering galaxy.

On the topmost shoot is fixed

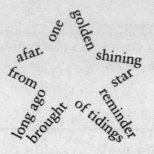

one golden shining star afar. from long ago brought of tidings reminder

Penny Kent

Maryland Christmas Tree

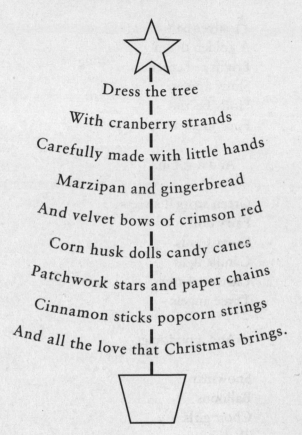

Dress the tree

With cranberry strands

Carefully made with little hands

Marzipan and gingerbread

And velvet bows of crimson red

Corn husk dolls candy canes

Patchwork stars and paper chains

Cinnamon sticks popcorn strings

And all the love that Christmas brings.

Anita Marie Sackett

The Advent Calendar

A silver ball
A golden drum
Bright red crackers
Shiny apples
Holly berries
Four jingle bells –

   And a robin.

Green striped sweets
Fairy doll
Santa Claus
Candle light
Christmas tree
Three angels –

   And a pudding.

Snowman
Balloons
Choir girls
Turkey
Reindeer –

   And a stocking.

Star
Kings
Gifts

AND A MANGER!

Rita Ray

Christmas Spirit

Friends

Katherine Gallagher

Home-made Cards

Making Christmas cards at home
Is difficult to do –
You need some scissors of your own
And lots and lots of glue.

You need bright stars upon their fronts
Or else they will be dull,
And you can make some snowmen too
From balls of cotton wool.

You need your crayons – green for trees
And red for Rudolph's nose,
And gold to light your candle up
So that it really glows.

Now sprinkle over everything
(plus house and babysitter)
the final, most important thing –
a little bit of glitter.

Clare Kirwan

Tree

Every year
you're here to light
the tinsel night.

In the corner of the room
your bright branches banish
winter's gloom.

I dress you carefully.
The bells, the baubles
glisten cheerfully.

Christmas tree.
You are my friend.
You'll be with me until
the old year's end.

Ann Bonner

A Happy Christmas

I'm dreaming of a HAPPY Christmas
everybody has a HAPPY face
war draws to an end
and enemies become friends
Yeah! Love embraces
the human race.

Levi Tafari

Christmas
(Acrostic)

Chill in the air,
Hoar frost,
Roaring wind,
Ice on the road,
Snow on the roof,
Travellers from afar.
Mother and child,
Angels in the sky,
Starlight.

Gervase Phinn

All Things White and Beautiful
(A Christmas song to the tune of 'All Things Bright and Beautiful')

All things white and beautiful
When snow begins to fall
Christmas time is wonderful
When Santa comes to call

The icicles on branches
The snowflakes on the ground
Silent snowmen smiling
And shining white around

All things white and beautiful . . .

Rudolph's nose is glowing
Santa's beard is white
Christmas stars are twinkling
On this special night

All things white and beautiful . . .

Lists have all been written
Stockings have been hung
Jingle bells are ringing
Carols have been sung

All things white and beautiful . . .

Every chimney's waiting
For that magic time
Every child is dreaming
Of what he'll leave behind

All things white and beautiful . . .

Paul Cookson

A Season of Peace

A
season
of peace
A season of
F
U
N
Joy to the world
for Christmas
has come

Celia Warren

Christmas Is Coming

Christmas is coming,
  The geese are getting fat,
Please to put a penny
  In the old man's hat.
If you haven't got a penny,
  A ha'penny will do;
If you haven't got a ha'penny,
  Then God bless you!

Anon.

The First Tree in the Greenwood

Now the holly bears a berry as white as the milk,
And Mary bore Jesus, who was wrapped up in silk:
And Mary bore Jesus Christ,
Our Saviour for to be,
And the first tree in the greenwood, it was the holly.

Now the holly bears a berry as green as the grass,
And Mary bore Jesus, who died on the cross:
And Mary bore Jesus Christ,
Our Saviour for to be,
And the first tree, in the greenwood, it was the holly.

Now the holly bears a berry as black as the coal
And Mary bore Jesus, who died for us all:
And Mary bore Jesus Christ,
Our Saviour for to be,
And the first tree in the greenwood, it was the holly.

Now the holly bears a berry, as blood is it red,
Then trust we our Saviour, who rose from the dead:
And Mary bore Jesus Christ,
Our Saviour for to be,
And the first tree in the greenwood, it was the holly.

Anon.

The Holly and the Ivy

The holly and the ivy –
One's prickly, one's not,
I sat down on the prickly one
And in the air I shot,

And shot up through the ceiling,
And shot up in the sky,
And wished a 'Merry Christmas' to
The pigeons passing by.

I shot above the rainbow,
And climbing towards heaven,
I wished a 'Merry Christmas' to
A Boeing 747.

I kept shooting higher
And higher, and soon
I was wishing 'Merry Christmas' to
The man in the moon.

Then I started to tumble
To fall back to earth,
To slow me down, I flapped my arms
For all that I was worth.

I fell back through the ceiling
And landed on a chair,
But luckily on a different one,
And the holly was not there.

So just you be careful
When Christmas comes round –
Be sure to check beneath you when
You're starting to sit down.

And just you remember
The thing I forgot:
The holly and the ivy –
One's prickly, one's not.

Richard Edwards

The Twelve Days of Christmas

On the first day of Christmas
My true love sent to me,
A partridge in a pear tree.

2. On the second day of Christmas
   My true love sent to me,
   Two turtle doves,
   And a partridge in a pear tree.

3. On the third day of Christmas
   My true love sent to me,
   Three French hens, two turtle doves
   And a partridge in a pear tree.

4. On the fourth day of Christmas
   My true love sent to me,
   Four calling birds, three French hens,
   Two turtle doves, and a partridge in a pear tree.

5. On the fifth day of Christmas
   My true love sent to me,
   Five gold rings, four calling birds, three French hens,
   Two turtle doves, and a partridge in a pear tree.

6. On the sixth day of Christmas
    My true love sent to me,
    Six geese a-laying, five gold rings,
    Four calling birds, three French hens,
    Two turtle doves, and a partridge in a pear tree.

7. On the seventh day of Christmas
    My true love sent to me
    Seven swans a-swimming,
    Six geese a-laying, etc.

8. On the eighth day of Christmas
    My true love sent to me,
    Eight maids a-milking,
    Seven swans a-swimming, etc.

9. On the ninth day of Christmas
    My true love sent to me,
    Nine drummers drumming,
    Eight maids a-milking, etc.

10. On the tenth day of Christmas
    My true love sent to me,
    Ten pipers piping,
    Nine drummers drumming, etc.

11. On the eleventh day of Christmas
    My true love sent to me,
    Eleven ladies dancing,
    Ten pipers piping, etc.

12. On the twelfth day of Christmas
    My true love sent to me,
    Twelve lords a-leaping,
    Eleven ladies dancing,
    Ten pipers piping,
    Nine drummers drumming,
    Eight maids a-milking
    Seven swans a-swimming,
    Six geese a-laying,
    Five gold rings,
    Four calling birds,
    Three French hens,
    Two turtle doves,
    And a partridge in a pear tree.

                                        Anon.

A Christmas Tree at Windsor

'My dear,' said Prince Albert, 'you seem to be
In a mood of the deepest glums.
Now I have an idea
That might help to cheer you
As Christmas comes.

'It's a custom back in my homeland,
A spruce or a fir – a small tree –
Hung with ribbons, bright papers,
All lit up with wax tapers:
I'll arrange it – that's if you agree.'

The Queen's voice was cool: 'My dear Albert,
I confess I'm a little confused.
Do you really desire
To set Windsor on fire?
We are definitely not amused.'

But ignoring the Queen's disapproval,
The Prince Consort, in great secrecy,
With their children, a maid
And some courtiers to aid,
Dressed a sumptuous Christmas tree . . .

A magical, glittering vision
As Victoria was brought on the scene;
Her eyes shone with delight
And her mood changed that night:
'We are greatly amused,' said the Queen.

Eric Finney

Christmas Party Invitation List

Greta Warmly
Honor Doorstep
Carol Singer
Belinda Hand
Donna Party-Hat
Ava Toddy
Paula Cracker
Buster Balloon
Cary Okey
Bob About
Dan Surround
Trudy Knight
Tilda Day
Mary Christmas

Philip Waddell

The Reverend Sabine Baring-Gould

The Reverend Sabine Baring-Gould,
    Rector (sometime) at Lew,
Once at a Christmas party asked,
    'Whose pretty child are you?'

(The Rector's family was long,
    His memory was poor,
And as to who was who had grown
    Increasingly unsure.)

At this, the infant on the stair
    Most sorrowfully sighed.
'Whose pretty little girl am I?
    Why, *yours*, papa!' she cried.

                    Charles Causley

In the Week When Christmas Comes

This is the week when Christmas comes,
Let every pudding burst with plums,
And every tree bear dolls and drums,
    In the week when Christmas comes.

Let every hall have boughs of green,
With berries glowing in between,
    In the week when Christmas comes.

Let every doorstep have a song
Sounding the dark street along,
    In the week when Christmas comes.

Let every steeple ring a bell
With a joyful tale to tell,
    In the week when Christmas comes.

Let every night put forth a star
To show us where the heavens are,
    In the week when Christmas comes.

Let every pen enfold a lamb
Sleeping warm beside its dam,
    In the week when Christmas comes.

This is the week when Christmas comes.

Eleanor Farjeon

A Week to Christmas

Sunday with six whole days to go,
How we'll endure it I don't know!

Monday the goodies are in the making,
Spice smells of pudding and mince pies a-baking.

Tuesday, Dad's home late and quiet as a mouse,
He smuggles packages into the house.

Wednesday's the day for decorating the tree,
Will the lights work again? We'll have to see.

Thursday's for last-minute shopping and hurry,
We've never seen Mum in quite such a flurry!

Friday is Christmas Eve when we lie awake
Trying to sleep before the day break.

And that special quiet on Christmas Morn
When far away in Bethlehem Christ was born.

John Cotton

Thomas's First Christingle

Thomas is holding
an orange world in his hand
and trying to keep
the candle on top upright.

He touches red ribbon, raisins, nuts
   – what's it all mean?
'The next bit's magic,'
his sister, Ann, whispers.
'Wait and see!'

In a big circle
all round the pews they stand:
mums, dads, children,
grandparents packed in tight.
One by one the candles are lit
and someone . . .
switches out the church lights!

In the darkness
the Christingle circle glows,
Christ's light
   shining on each single face.

                Patricia Leighton

The Christmas Secret

One year, I made a wish so secret,
So precious
I would not write it down,
Or call it from my window,
Or whisper it to the moon.
Instead I spoke it in my mind
Over and over
As Christmas crept closer.

My friends teased and prodded,
My parents leaned down
With questions that smelled of
Puddings and pies,
The High Street Father Christmas
Searched for clues in my eyes,
But my wish could not be found
In any shop or shiny catalogue.

'The REAL Santa will know,'
I told myself
While the other children
Roared their demands
Like small emperors
And stamped their fierce feet.

On Christmas morning
All the proper presents
Bulged in my stocking
Or loomed beside my bed,
But I slipped past them to stand
Breathless with hope
On the frosty doorstep.

And there were the boot-prints
Marching across silver grass.
There was the tangle of red thread
Caught in our holly bush,
There was the faint jingle of bells
On the winter air –
And there, in the cold fingers
Of our apple tree
Was my secret gift.

In a moment it melted and fluttered away
As softly as a white owl's feather,
And I turned back to the indoor world
Of toast and cosy surprises.

But the magic has stayed with me
To this far, grown-up day,
And now it is time to loosen its ribbon of stars
And share it with you.

Clare Bevan

Christmas Eve

On Christmas Eve
it is so late
that even Mum and Dad
are fast asleep in bed.

I stand at the top of the stairs.

The house is warm
and the tree lights glow.

I can smell mince pies
and anticipation.

I make a wish.

Roger Stevens

Too Excited

Tonight I'm too excited
To try and get to sleep
Mum and Dad have told me
To try by counting sheep
Instead I'm counting reindeer
Their noses glowing red
Each one I count just makes me
More wide awake instead
The more I count, the closer
Santa seems to be
And I just love the magic
And the mystery

Paul Cookson

Beds

I like it in my roomy bed.
It's friendly and it's neat.
It gently holds my sleepy head
And rests my weary feet.
A handsome, coloured quilt on top
A mattress warm down under.
And yet . . . around a bed of straw
The world once stood in wonder.

Max Fatchen

Christmas Eve

Our
pud is
cooked,
meat stuffed and rolled –
smells drift of fruit and almonds where
the cake is iced and waiting.

Our tree is up, green, red and gold,
and twists of tinsel shimmer there
from lights illuminating.

Our foil-wrapped secrets to unfold,
and tiptoe stockings hung with care,
are all at once creating

A feeling that we want to hold
suspended in the tingling air –

**It's
called
anticipating.**

Liz Brownlee

A Visit from St Nicholas

'Twas the night before Christmas, when all through the house
Not a creature was stirring, not even a mouse;
The stockings were hung by the chimney with care,
In hopes that St Nicholas soon would be there;
The children were nestled all snug in their beds,
While visions of sugar-plums danced in their heads;
And mamma in her 'kerchief, and I in my cap,
Had just settled our brains for a long winter's nap –
When out on the lawn there arose such a clatter,
I sprang from my bed to see what was the matter.
Away to the window I flew like a flash,
Tore open the shutters, and threw up the sash.
The moon, on the breast of the new-fallen snow,
Gave the lustre of midday to objects below;
When, what to my wondering eyes should appear,
But a miniature sleigh and eight tiny reindeer,
With a little old driver, so lively and quick,
I knew in a moment it must be St Nick.
More rapid than eagles his coursers they came,
And he whistled, and shouted, and called them by name:
'Now, *Dasher*! now, *Dancer*! now, *Prancer* and *Vixen*!
On, *Comet*! on, *Cupid*! on, *Donder* and *Blitzen*!
To the top of the porch! to the top of the wall!
Now dash away! dash away! dash away all!'
As dry leaves that before the wild hurricane fly,
When they meet with an obstacle, mount to the sky;
So up to the house-top the coursers they flew
With the sleigh full of toys, and St Nicholas too.

72

And then, in a twinkling, I heard on the roof
The prancing and pawing of each little hoof –
As I drew in my head, and was turning around,
Down the chimney St Nicholas came with a bound.
He was dressed all in fur, from his head to his foot,
And his clothes were all tarnished with ashes and soot;
A bundle of toys he had flung on his back,
And he looked like a pedlar just opening his pack.
His eyes – how they twinkled; his dimples, how merry!
His cheeks were like roses, his nose like a cherry!
His droll little mouth was drawn up like a bow,
And the beard of his chin was as white as the snow;
The stump of a pipe he held tight in his teeth,
And the smoke it encircled his head like a wreath;
He had a broad face and a little round belly
That shook, when he laughed, like a bowl full of jelly.
He was chubby and plump, a right jolly old elf,
And I laughed when I saw him, in spite of myself;
A wink of his eye and a twist of his head
Soon gave me to know I had nothing to dread;
He spoke not a word, but went straight to his work,
And filled all the stockings; then turned with a jerk,
And laying his fingers aside of his nose,
And giving a nod, up the chimney he rose;
He sprang to his sleigh, to his team gave a whistle,
And away they all flew like the down of a thistle.
But I heard him exclaim, ere he drove out of sight,
'*Happy Christmas to all, and to all a good night!*'

Clement Clarke Moore

73

All Through The House
(Not A Creature Was Stirring)
(After Clement Clarke Moore)

'Twas the night before Christmas,
And all through the house,
Not a creature was stirring,
Not even a mouse.

Not even a squirrel,
Not even a rat,
Not even a herring,
Not even a sprat.

From front door to back door,
From basement to roof,
Not an animal moved,
Not a paw, not a hoof.

Not a tail, not a claw,
Not a tentacle stirred.
No animal noises at all
Could be heard.

Not a roar, not a growl,
Not a tweet nor a squeak.
Not a hiss nor a moo,
Not a bark nor a shriek.

There was no sign at all
Of a badger or bear;
Not a fox in the hall,
And no shark on the stair.

Not a fish, not a fowl,
Neither reptile nor mammal,
Not one single rhino,
Not one single camel.

While outside, the snow
Drifted round like a blizzard,
Inside, nothing stirred,
Not a pig, not a lizard.

Not one elephant moved,
Not a mole or chinchilla;
Not one giant bat,
Not one mountain gorilla.

All that Christmas Eve night
Still not one creature stirred.
Not one horse in the house,
Not one whale could be heard.

Not a wallaby moved.
Not a leopard or squid.
They were all keeping still,
And all keeping well hid.

And so all through the night
As the family slumbered,
Still not one creature cantered
Or galloped or lumbered

Or scampered or clambered
Or slithered or crept
Or waddled or fluttered
Or lolloped or leapt.

And even as day broke,
And right up *until*
All the family woke,
All the beasts kept quite still . . .

Then, as one, they leapt out
And all yelled, without warning:
'HAPPY CHRISTMAS TO ALL,
AND TO ALL, A GOOD MORNING!'

David Bateman

Christmas Eve

Nearly midnight;
still can't sleep!
Has he been yet?
Dare I peep?

Sneak out softly,
creaking floor!
Down the stairs
and through the door . . .
In the darkness
by the tree,
tightly wrapped . . .
but which for me?
Feel the ribbon,
find the card!
This one? That one?
Heart thumps hard.
Trembling fingers,
throbbing head,
then . . .

a voice yells

BACK TO BED!

Judith Nicholls

Christmas Express

It's a perfect night for flying,
the moon is full and gold.
The stars shine out from darkest blue;
there are presents in the hold.

It's a perfect night for flying,
and the pilot's feeling jolly.
The cockpit's decked in tinsel
and mistletoe and holly.

It's a perfect night for flying.
The air is cold and bright.
We hurtle through the stratosphere –
we all enjoy the flight.

It's a perfect night for flying,
we're singing as we go.
We can hear a thousand voices
joining in from far below.

It's a perfect night for flying,
but the sky is broad and steep,
so when this reindeer's home, he'll spend
his Christmas Day asleep.

Alison Chisholm

A Jolly Old Fellow in Red

A jolly old fellow in red
set his reindeer on full speed ahead
and all in one night,
faster than light,
left presents round everyone's bed.

Marian Swinger

A Naughty Boy Tale

A boy I know called Sammy Day
once discovered Santa's sleigh
parked beside a Christmas tree
– while Santa went to have some tea.
Sam looked around – and by the door
he spied a sack upon the floor:
'His present sack!' he cried in glee!
'That's just the sort of thing for me!'
and with a laugh and robber's shout
he took it home to sort it out.
'What a prize!' he grinned in glee.
'Lots of presents all for me!'
and with a shake of bag and head,
he emptied it upon his bed.
'Oh no!' he gasped!
– oh, what a shock –
for out fell
piles of pants and socks, a bobbled hat, a bright
red coat, some SHIRTS, some VESTS, and
POWDERED SOAP!
A note inside:

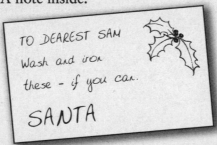

TO DEAREST SAM
Wash and iron
these – if you can.

SANTA

Peter Dixon

Missing Ingredient

Bobble hat
White beard
Red jacket
Fat tummy
Shiny sleigh
Fast reindeer
Juicy carrots
Yummy yummy
Latest book on chimney climbing
Sack of presents
Lots of snow

At last
All ready
Hang on . . .

where's my HO HO HO?

Andrea Shavick

Christmas Kenning

Rooftop hopper,
Cloud topper,
Wildwind rider,
Snow slider,
Dream carrier,
Starlight courier,
Blizzard breaker,
Present taker,
Reindeer trailer,
Silver sailor,
Santa's sleigh.

Tim Pointon

Christmas Present

Wrote my Christmas letter to Santa
In the leafy month of June
If you want a football for Christmas
You can never write too soon.

I pestered my sister every day:
'Do you think my football will come?'
She shrugged and told me to ask my dad
And Dad said, 'Ask your mum.'

Oh the months they slide like snails it seems
And there's hundreds of hours in each day
So I wrote two more letters just in case
My first had gone astray.

But finally Christmas Eve came round
And I tried not to fall asleep
While over the houses and hedges and streets
The snow lay soft and deep.

It was dawn on Christmas morning
When I finally raised my head
And saw my football nestling
At the bottom of the bed.

On the roof the sound of reindeer hooves
Cantering over the snow
And the voice of an old man singing,
'Here we go, here we go, here we go.'

Gareth Owen

Welcome Yule

Now, thrice welcome Christmas,
  Which brings us good cheer,
Minced pies and plum porridge,
  Good ale and strong beer;
With pig, goose, and capon,
  The best that can be,
So well doth the weather
  And our stomachs agree.

Observe how the chimneys
  Do smoke all about,
The cooks are providing
  For dinner no doubt;
But those on whose tables
  No victuals appear,
O may they keep Lent
  All the rest of the year!

With holly and ivy
  So green and so gay,
We deck up our houses
  As fresh as the day.
With bays and rosemary,
  And laurel complete;
And everyone now
  Is a king in conceit.

George Wither

Christmas Morning

early on
everything frosted like iron
we woke, my brother and I,
to the creak on the stair
and silently
pumped up like balloons
with excitement
we pretended sleep
until Santa (or Mum or Dad)
had gone –

ducked our heads into Christmas
pillowsacks of –

crackly paper
oranges and apples sweet and tangy
chocolate money
plastic made-in-Hong-Kong rockets
sheriffs badge
pair of socks (from Auntie May, handknitted)
a colouring book
and pencils that smell of Friday afternoons in school
a bag of dinosaurs, red, blue, brown and green
a false nose
a set of magic tricks
a crêpe paper cracker with glossy band
a rattly handful of walnuts at the bottom
a thread of cotton
a few sparks of glitter . . .

I wish I could live inside here
forever!

Stephen Bowkett

Christmas Stocking

What will go into the Christmas Stocking
While the clock on the mantelpiece goes tick-tocking?
    An orange, a penny,
    Some sweets, not too many,
    A trumpet, a dolly,
    A sprig of red holly,
    A book and a top
    And a grocery shop,
    Some beads in a box,
    An ass and an ox
    And a lamb, plain and good,
    All whittled in wood,
    A white sugar dove,
    A handful of love,
    Another of fun,
    And it's very near done –
    A big silver star
    On top – there you are!
Come morning you'll wake to the clock's tick-tocking,
And that's what you'll find in the Christmas Stocking.

Eleanor Farjeon

The Zoo Creatures' Christmas

When Santa reached the City Zoo
He knew EXACTLY what to do –
He sorted through his sack and sleigh
And left some treats for Christmas Day . . .

Ginger socks for the desert fox,
Colourful ties for the butterflies,
Soft, grey gloves for the turtle doves,
Furry bloomers for chilly pumas,
Big brassieres for the grizzly bears,
Slinky frocks for the lady crocs,
Enormous shoes for the kangaroos,
Tiny pants for the soldier ants,
Royal dresses for the lionesses,
Velvet capes for elegant apes,
Small, red hats for the vampire bats,
Stripy suits for the bandicoots,
Petticoats for the nanny goats,
An extra-long scarf for the old giraffe,
Slim, black hose for the carrion crows,
Toppers and tails for the snooty snails,
Comfy slippers for sea lion flippers,
And warm pyjamas for sleepy llamas.

So – did the creatures cheer and purr?
And were they pleased? Of course they were!

Clare Bevan

The Colour of Christmas

On Christmas morning
everything's white,
Santa brought snowflakes
when he came in the night.

On Christmas afternoon
everything's red,
ribbons and candles,
berries high overhead.

On Christmas evening
everything's green,
like our tree in the corner,
the tallest you've seen.

On Christmas night
everything's black,
moon shadows, the sky,
Santa's huge empty sack.

Moira Andrew

Christmas Morning

Last year
On Christmas morning
We got up really early
And took the dog for a walk
Across the downs

It wasn't snowing
But the hills were white with frost
And our breath froze
In the air

Judy rushed around like a crazy thing
As though Christmas
meant something special to her

The sheep huddled together
looking tired
as if they'd been up all night
watching the stars

We stood at the highest point
And thought about what Christmas means
And looked over the white hills
And looked up at the blue sky

And the hills seemed
To go on forever
And the sky had no bounds
And you could imagine
A world at peace

Roger Stevens

Father to Son

For Christmas, give me a rare thing:
A meteorite fallen from space –
(I don't care if it's really a marble) –
Or a map of a secret place
Where X marks the spot, or some seaweed,
Or a snake-shaped stick, or a snail shell you've found,
Or one of your drawings of fish men,
Or the shape of your funny feet traced from the ground,
Or a spell, or some mud from a puddle
Wrapped up in a leaky box,
But please
Please please
Please please
Please please
Please please
Don't give me
Socks.

Richard Edwards

A Happy Christmas

Christmas day. The tree is bright
with tiny dots of coloured light.
The turkey's ready. What a sight.
Take the first delicious bite.
Snowflakes falling. Well they might
cover the world in sparkling white.
All day without a single fight.
Everything has been just right.
Family round the fireside, quite
sleepy now. It's Christmas night.

Geraldine Aldridge

The Ascent of Everest

On the last afternoon of the holidays
We three intrepid mountaineers
Climbed Everest – again;

We'd already done it in the morning.

But, this time by the most difficult route,
Across the South Ridge
And up the treacherous North Face;

The side by the banisters.

Once again, Chris Bonington (that's me)
Little Jack and Samantha our faithful guide,
Struggled across the endless foothills,

By the telephone table.

Then huddled together, we stood staring up
Through the late afternoon mists,
At the fearful white cliff

Of the upstairs toilet door.

And so we set off up the Great Glacier.
Pausing only once, flat against the ice wall,
To let another solitary mountaineer squeeze by,

To get to the loo.

Then at last – halfway up – Camp 6,
We stopped, nearly exhausted;
Just long enough to catch our breath

And eat our smoky-bacon crisps and Smarties.

Then on, climbing, climbing ever upwards,
For the final assult on the summit.
At last, we stood on the roof of the world.

Up there by the landing radiator.

Hugs and handshakes all round,
And three hearty cheers.
Then, it was Samantha's turn to plant the flag

In the vase on the window sill.

Then down, down, the icy slopes.
A brief stop at Camp 6 to collect our litter.

Finally, on to base camp, civilization and,

Into the kitchen for Coke, Kit-Kats and – Kathmandu.

David Whitehead

The Lost Pantomime

Where's the pantomime?
It's behind you!
Oh no it isn't!
Oh yes it is!

Nick Toczek

Pantomime Poem

I'm going to write a pantomime poem
OH NO YOU'RE NOT!
Oh yes I am!
One that will get everyone going
OH NO YOU'RE NOT!
Oh yes I am!

There'll be huge custard pies
And girls who slap thighs,
Men dressed in frocks
And bloomers with dots,
There'll be beanstalks and castles,
Some heroes, some rascals.
There'll be goodies to sing to
And villains BEHIND YOU!
There'll be eggs that are golden
An actor who's an old 'un!
Cows all called Daisy
And songs that are crazy!

I'm going to write a pantomime poem
OH NO YOU'RE NOT!
Oh yes I am!
One that will get everyone going
OH NO YOU'RE NOT!
Oh yes I am!
OH NO YOU'RE NOT!
Oh yes I am!
OH NO YOU'RE NOT!
I just did!!

Coral Rumble

Toboggan

Take me where the snow lies deep
On some hillside high and steep.
Boldly sit astride my sleigh
One good push and I'm away.
Going speeding down the hill.
Getting faster – What a thrill!
At the bottom brush off snow.
Now to the top for another go.

David Whitehead

Starfall

Exploded stars,
   cosmos swirled,
     each winter fall
       upon our world.

This dust of stars,
   weightless, white,
     drifts down and settles
       in the night.

We wake to find
   the fields aglow,
     and wrongly call
       this starfall . . . snow.

Wes Magee

Snowflakes

Snowflakes are falling
as soft as pussy-willows.
Perhaps it's the Snow-Queen
shaking out her pillows.

It might be showers of stardust
falling from the sky,
or a little fluffy cloud
who's just started to cry.

Or drips of ice-cream dripping from
a giant's ice-cream cone,
or scales from an ice-dragon
flying all alone.

Or feathers from a swan
flying to the frozen lake,
or maybe Father Christmas
is icing a cake.

Could it be white leaves dropping
from rice-paper trees?
No. It's all the Christmas Fairies,
dancing on the breeze!

Geraldine Aldridge

Christmas Haiku

In the hot kitchen,
fresh mince pies with sugared crusts –
outside, falling snow.

Penny Kent

Remembering Snow

I did not sleep last night.
The falling snow was beautiful and white.
I went downstairs,
And opened wide the door.
I had not seen such snow before.
Our grubby little street had gone –
All looked brand new, and everywhere
There was a pureness in the air.
I felt such peace. Watching every flake
I felt more and more awake.
I thought I'd learned all there was to know
About the trillion million different kinds
Of swirling frosty flakes of falling snow.
But that was not so.
I did not know how vividly it lit
The world with such a peaceful glow.
Upstairs my parents slept.
I could not drag myself away from that sight
To call them down and have them share
The mute miracle of the snow.
It seemed to fall for me alone.
How beautiful our little street had grown!

Brian Patten

Snowflake Chant

Two, four, six, eight,
Think I saw a snowflake – great!
Eight, two, four, six,
Snowing harder – hope it sticks!
Six, eight, two, four,
Keep on snowing – more, more, MORE!
Four, six, eight, two,
Sledges out and join the queue!

Sue Cowling

Winter

Frost curls, ice creeps
Over lake, still and deep.
Bracken's flat, dying red,
Frost's curling overhead.
Twinkling hill tops, flakes of snow,
Starving seagulls swooping low.
Breath frosts, feet stamp.
House warm, world damp.
Toes glow, baths steam,
Santa Claus, reindeer dream.
Christmas trees, cards and bells,
Snow melts, river swells.
Water freezing, skates out,

Roaring fire, gathering about.
Cribs are lit, church bells chime,
Windows glow at Christmas time.
Warm pyjamas, bed snug,
Cuddled up in winter's hug.
Think of mugs of steaming drink,
Santa's sleigh bells chime and chink.
Owls hunt, trees stand bare,
Snow blankets everywhere.
Cosy evenings, frosty days,
Watery sun in misty haze.
Patchwork quilts, polar bears,
Woolly winter underwear.

Julia Rawlinson
(written aged 10)

Country, All the Winter Long

But
not
yet,
the
ice
in
the   cow
           trod
           lane
                    Lingers.

But
spring hints,
new
bud
and
a leaf.

All
chilblains
and
flu
and
colds.

Oct
Nov frosts.
Dec
Jan
Feb
March

The winter cold,
Snows   white.
Black   skies,
Fires,   rockets,
Thick woollens,
Icy pathways.
Nose   runny,
Toes   frozen.
Scarf   cosy,
Oven   warm.
Trees   bare,
The winter is cold.

Eric Petrie

A Winter Night

One night when the sky is clear
and there's no moon
and the stars are like
a scattering of snow sparkle
and the ponds are frozen
and there's no room
at any inn

and you can't cycle
because of the sheet ice,
you will walk home
in the lonely dark
thinking about those blazing
logs on the fire
you know will be waiting

and your breath will curl
from your mouth like smoke
and even in your pockets
your gloved hands
will be freezing.

That night you will stare
up at the Great Bear
or Orion or the Pole Star
and make a promise.
And you will keep it;
keep it for ever.

Gerard Benson

Almost New Year

It's the last afternoon
of the old year
and already a full fat moon
is in charge of the sky.
It has nudged the sun
into a distant lake
and left it to drown,
while bare branch trees
like blackened fireworks
burst with sunset.
Frost is patterning the fields,
a tractor tries to furrow
the iron hard hill.
Winter's frown settles
on the face of the landscape.
It shrugs its shoulders,
gives in to January.

Brian Moses

The New Year

I am the little New Year, ho, ho!
Here I come tripping it over the snow.
Shaking my bells with a merry din –
So open your doors and let me in!

Presents I bring for each and all –
Big folks, little folks, short and tall;
Each one from me a treasure may win –
So open your doors and let me in!

Some shall have silver and some shall have gold,
Some shall have new clothes and some shall have old;
Some shall have brass and some shall have tin –
So open your doors and let me in!

Some shall have water and some shall have milk,
Some shall have satin and some shall have silk!
But each from me a present may win –
So open your doors and let me in!

Anon.

Good Riddance But Now What?

Come, children, gather round my knee;
Something is about to be.

Tonight's December thirty-first,
Something is about to burst.

The clock is crouching, dark and small,
Like a time bomb in the hall.

Hark! It's midnight, children dear.
Duck! Here comes another year.

Ogden Nash

Christmas Carols and Songs

Silent Night

1. Si - lent night, Ho - ly

night, All is calm,

all is bright; Round the

Vir - gin Mo - ther and Child,

Ho - ly in - fant so ten - der and

mild, Sleep in hea - ven - ly

peace, _____ Sleep_ in

hea - ven - ly peace._____

2. Silent night, Holy night,
   Shepherds quake at the sight;
   Glories stream from heaven afar,
   Heavenly hosts sing Alleluya:
   Christ the Saviour is born,
   Christ the Saviour is born.

3. Silent night, Holy night,
   Son of God, love's pure light;
   Radiance beams from thy holy face,
   With the dawn of redeeming grace;
   Jesus, Lord, at thy birth,
   Jesus, Lord, at thy birth.

Once in Royal David's City

2. He came down to earth from heaven
   Who is God and Lord of all,
   And his shelter was a stable,
   And his cradle was a stall;
   With the poor and mean and lowly
   Lived on earth our Saviour holy.

3. And through all his wondrous childhood
   He would honour and obey,
   Love and watch the lowly maiden,
   In whose gentle arms he lay;
   Christian children all must be
   Mild, obedient, good as he.

4. For he is our childhood's pattern,
   Day by day like us he grew,
   He was little, weak, and helpless,
   Tears and smiles like us he knew;
   And he feeleth for our sadness,
   And he shareth in our gladness.

5. And our eyes at last shall see him,
   Through his own redeeming love,
   For that child so dear and gentle
   Is our Lord in heaven above;
   And he leads his children on
   To the place where he is gone.

6. Not in that poor lowly stable,
   With the oxen standing by,
   We shall see him, but in heaven,
   Set at God's right hand on high;
   Where like stars his children crowned
   All in white shall wait around.

Ding Dong Merrily on High

1. Ding dong mer - ri - ly on high! In
heav'n the bells are ring - ing.
Ding dong ve - ri - ly the sky Is
riv'n with an - gels sing - ing:

CHORUS

Glo - - -

- - - - -

2. E'en so here below, below
    Let steeple bells be swungen.
    And i-o, i-o, i-o
    By priest and people sungen:
      Gloria, Hosanna in excelsis!
      Gloria, Hosanna in excelsis!

3. Pray you, dutifully prime
    Your matin chime, ye ringers;
    May you beautifully rime
    Your evetime song, ye singers:
      Gloria, Hosanna in excelsis!
      Gloria, Hosanna in excelsis!

Deck the Hall

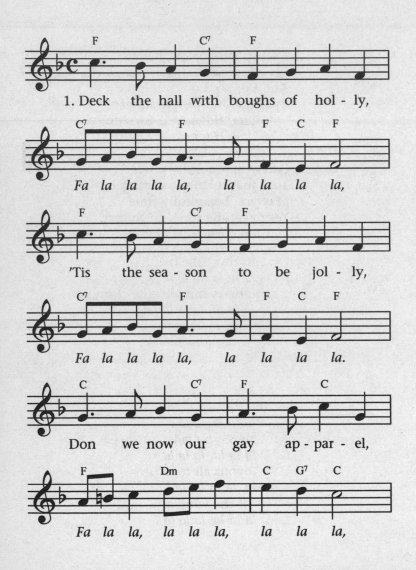

1. Deck the hall with boughs of hol - ly,

Fa la la la la, la la la la,

'Tis the sea - son to be jol - ly,

Fa la la la la, la la la la.

Don we now our gay ap - par - el,

Fa la la, la la la, la la la,

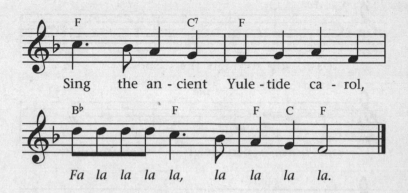

Sing the an - cient Yule - tide ca - rol,

Fa la la la la, la la la la.

2. See the blazing Yule before us,
   Fu lu lu la la, la la la la,
   Strike the harp and join the chorus,
   Fa la la la la, la la la la.
   Follow me in merry measure,
   Fa la la, la la la, la la la,
   While I tell of Yuletide treasure,
   Fa la la la la, la la la la.

3. Fast away the old year passes,
   Fa la la la la, la la la la,
   Hail the new, you lads and lasses,
   Fa la la la la, la la la la.
   Sing we joyous all together,
   Fa la la, la la la, la la la,
   Heedless of the wind and weather,
   Fa la la la la, la la la la.

Jingle Bells

Hark! the Herald Angels Sing

1. Hark! the he - rald an - gels sing__

Glo - ry to the new - born King,

Peace on earth and mer - cy mild, __

God and sin - ners re - con - ciled.

Joy - ful all ye na - tions rise, __

Join the tri - umph of the skies;

With th'an-gel - ic host pro - claim:

'Christ is born in Beth - le - hem'.

Hark! the he - rald an - gels sing

Glo - ry to the new - born King.

2. Christ, by highest Heav'n adored,
   Christ, the Everlasting Lord,
   Late in time behold him come,
   Offspring of a virgin's womb.
   Veiled in flesh the Godhead see,
   Hail the incarnate Deity!
   Pleased as Man with man to dwell,
   Jesus, our Emmanuel.
   Hark! the herald angels sing
   Glory to the newborn King.

3. Hail, the heaven-born Prince of Peace!
   Hail, the Sun of Righteousness!
   Light and life to all he brings,
   Risen with healing in his wings.
   Mild he lays his glory by,
   Born that man no more may die,
   Born to raise the sons of earth,
   Born to give them second birth.
   Hark! the herald angels sing
   Glory to the newborn King.

The Little Drummer Boy

1. 'Come', they told me, Pa -
rum pa - pum - pum,_____

'Our new - born King to see! Pa -
- rum - pa - pum - pum,_____

Our fin - est gifts we bring, Pa -
- rum - pa - pum - pum,_____

To lay be - fore the King! Pa -

-rum - pa - pum - pum, Rum - pa - pum - pum,

rum - pa - pum - pum,_____

So to hon - our Him, Pa -

- rum - pa - pum - pum,_____

When we come.'_____

2. 'Little Baby, Pa-rum-pa-pum-pum,
   I am a poor boy too, Pa-rum-pa-pum-pum,
   I have no gift to bring, Pa-rum-pa-pum-pum,
   That's fit to give our King! Pa-rum-pa-pum-pum,
   Rum-pa-pum-pum, rum-pa-pum-pum,
   Shall I play for You, Pa-rum-pa-pum-pum,
   On my drum?'

3. Mary nodded, Pa-rum-pa-pum-pum,
   The ox and lamb kept time, Pa-rum-pa-pum-pum,
   I played my drum for Him, Pa-rum-pa-pum-pum,
   I played my best for Him, Pa-rum-pa-pum-pum,
   Rum-pa-pum-pum, rum-pa-pum-pum,
   Then He smiled at me, Pa-rum-pa-pum-pum,
   Me and my drum!

The Holly and the Ivy

1. The hol-ly and the i-vy, When they are both full grown, Of___ all the trees that are in the wood, The__ hol-ly bears the crown. O *The ris-ing of the sun___ And the run-ning of the deer, The___*

CHORUS

play - ing of the mer - ry or - gan, Sweet

sing - ing in the choir.

2. The holly bears a blossom,
   As white as any flower,
   And Mary bore sweet Jesus Christ
   To be our sweet Saviour:
       O The rising of the sun
       And the running of the deer,
       The playing of the merry organ,
       Sweet singing in the choir.

3. The holly bears a berry,
   As red as any blood,
   And Mary bore sweet Jesus Christ
   To do poor sinners good:
       O The rising of the sun
       And the running of the deer,
       The playing of the merry organ,
       Sweet singing in the choir.

4. The holly bears a prickle,
   As sharp as any thorn,
   And Mary bore sweet Jesus Christ
   On Christmas day in the morn:
   > *O The rising of the sun*
   > *And the running of the deer,*
   > *The playing of the merry organ,*
   > *Sweet singing in the choir.*

5. The holly bears a bark,
   As bitter as any gall,
   And Mary bore sweet Jesus Christ
   For to redeem us all:
   > *O The rising of the sun*
   > *And the running of the deer,*
   > *The playing of the merry organ,*
   > *Sweet singing in the choir.*

6. The holly and the ivy,
   When they are both full grown,
   Of all the trees that are in the wood,
   The holly bears the crown:
   > *O The rising of the sun*
   > *And the running of the deer,*
   > *The playing of the merry organ,*
   > *Sweet singing in the choir.*

I Saw Three Ships

1. I saw three ships come sail-ing in, On
Christ - mas Day, on Christ - mas Day, I
saw three ships come sail - ing in On
Christ - mas Day in the morn - ing.

2. And what was in those ships all three?
   On Christmas Day, on Christmas Day,
   And what was in those ships all three?
   On Christmas day in the morning.

3. Our Saviour Christ and his lady.
   On Christmas Day, on Christmas Day,
   Our Saviour Christ and his lady.
   On Christmas day in the morning.

4. Pray, whither sailed those ships all three?
On Christmas Day, on Christmas Day,
Pray, whither sailed those ships all three?
On Christmas day in the morning.

5. O, they sailed into Bethlehem.
On Christmas Day, on Christmas Day,
O, they sailed into Bethlehem.
On Christmas day in the morning.

6. And all the bells on earth shall ring.
On Christmas Day, on Christmas Day,
And all the bells on earth shall ring.
On Christmas day in the morning.

7. And all the angels in Heaven shall sing.
On Christmas Day, on Christmas Day,
And all the angels in Heaven shall sing.
On Christmas day in the morning.

8. And all the souls on earth shall sing.
On Christmas Day, on Christmas Day,
And all the souls on earth shall sing.
On Christmas day in the morning.

9. Then let us all rejoice amain!
On Christmas Day, on Christmas Day,
Then let us all rejoice amain!
On Christmas day in the morning.

O Little Town of Bethlehem

1. O lit-tle town of Beth-le-hem, How still we__ see thee lie! A - bove thy deep and dream-less__ sleep The si - lent__ stars go by: Yet__ in thy dark streets shi - neth The

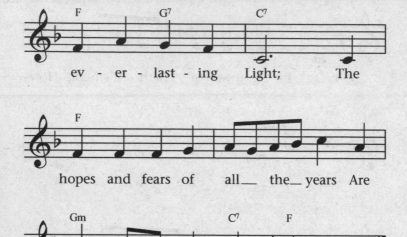

ev - er - last - ing   Light;   The

hopes and fears of   all__ the__ years Are

met   in__   thee   to - night.

2. For Christ is born of Mary;
   And, gathered all above,
   While mortals sleep, the angels keep
   Their watch of wondering love.
   O, morning stars, together
   Proclaim the holy birth,
   And praises sing to God the King
   And peace to men on earth.

3. How silently, how silently,
   The wondrous gift is given!
   So God imparts to human hearts
   The blessings of his heaven.
   No ear may hear his coming;
   But in this world of sin,
   Where meek souls will receive him, still
   The dear Christ enters in.

4. O holy Child of Bethlehem,
   Descend to us, we pray;
   Cast out our sin, and enter in:
   Be born in us today.
   We hear the Christmas angels
   The great glad tidings tell:
   O come to us, abide with us,
   Our Lord Emmanuel.

Plays for Christmas

The Nativity

by Pie Corbett

Characters

The Angel Gabriel
Mary
Narrator
Cat
Joseph
Donkey

Sleepy Innkeeper
Angry Innkeeper
Kind Innkeeper
Dog

Shepherd 1
Shepherd 2
Shepherd 3
Sheep 1
Sheep 2
King 1
King 2
King 3
Camel 1
Camel 2
Camel 3
Herod
Mouse
Angels (non-speaking)
Stars (non-speaking)
Sheep (non-speaking)

SCENE 1:   The Angel appears to Mary

Mary is in the centre of the stage sewing.

Narrator: Welcome to our nativity play. This is the story of how a great King was born in a poor stable. It happened two thousand years ago and we have not forgotten to retell the story.
This year it will be told by the animals.
The animals who were there.
The animals who saw it all.
The animals, both great and small.

A troupe of stars/angels appear and dance round Mary. She kneels down in prayer. A cat is sitting at the side of the stage, cleaning its paws and watching.

Cat: I was there. I saw it all. Mary was sweeping the kitchen floor when an angel appeared, bright as the sun. At first she was afraid but then the angel spoke in a voice made of starlight.

Angel Gabriel:
Do not be afraid. God has chosen you to have his baby. He will become the greatest of Kings and his world will last forever.

The angels and stars exit and Joseph enters.

Joseph: Are you all right, Mary?

Mary: Something amazing has happened. An angel spoke to me. I am to have a baby and he will become a great King.

Joseph: I know. I dreamed about this last night. We have to call him Jesus – which means – the one who saves.

Narrator: But there was a problem. They had to travel south to Bethlehem, for the Romans were making a list of everyone's names. So they set off, with Mary riding a donkey.

    Mary and Joseph plus donkey circle the stage or walk through the audience, if there is space, on their way to Bethlehem. The cat can follow too.

Donkey: I was there. I saw it all.
We rode across the hot, dusty plains and wandered beneath the great stars.
In the heat of the day, we took shelter.
In the cool of the morning, we walked.
But with each step,
God shone his light on us.

    As they move round, the Choir sings 'Little Donkey'. (Words and music on page 155.)

SCENE 2: **Arriving at the Inn**

> *On the side of the stage are three innkeepers,*
> *sitting on stools behind imaginary doors. Mary*
> *and Joseph and the donkey walk from door to*
> *door, knocking at each one.*

Joseph   [*Knock, knock, knock on door 1.*]

Sleepy Innkeeper [*yawning and stretching*]:
> What do you want?

Joseph: Is there any room?

Sleepy Innkeeper:
> Sorry, mate, no room here.

Joseph   [*Knock, knock, knock on door 2.*]

Angry Innkeeper [*snapping*]:
> What do you want?

Joseph: Is there any room?

Angry Innkeeper:
> No room here! And stop all that knocking. It's
> keeping me awake! Why, I cannot sleep a wink
> with you lot banging about down here.

Joseph, Mary, Donkey and Cat sit down centre stage – head in hands in despair.
The Choir sings 'There Isn't Any Room'. (Words and music on page 158.)

Joseph: I'll try once more. [*Softly, knock, knock, knock on door 3.*]

Kind Innkeeper:
It's late and I'm tired. What do you need? So far from home and all alone.

Joseph: Is there any room?

Kind Innkeeper:
Sorry, mate, no room here. But you can sleep round the back.

Joseph, Mary, the donkey and Cat move to the centre-left and back of the stage where they sit in the 'stable'. There is a cradle in front of them. A dog is lying in the far corner. It gets up and watches.

Dog: I was there. I saw it all.
From the cold corner
In a stable,
In a stall,
When the stars
Began to fall.

In a place
Fit for sheep.
There the baby
Lay asleep.

The Choir sings 'Away in a Manger'. (Words and music on page 160.)

SCENE 3: The Shepherds and the Kings

Narrator: That night three shepherds were looking after their sheep on a hillside near Bethlehem.

Three shepherds and a few sheep wander on to the front of the stage and sit down. They discuss their sheep and poke the fire. The stable scene is at the back of the stage – with everyone keeping as still as possible!

Shepherd 1:
The hill is still. It's cold tonight.

Shepherd 2 [*pointing across stage*]:
But in the East, a distant light.

Shepherd 3:
And voices too, like stars in flight.

A string of angels and stars dances on and creates a semi-circle around the shepherds.

149

Angel Gabriel:

> Do not be afraid. A baby has been born in
> Bethlehem. He will be King of all.
> You will find him lying in a manger.

Sheep 1:

> I was there. I saw it all –
> Follow your dream,
> Over the hill.
> Follow the star,
> While the night is still.

Sheep 2:

> I was there. I saw it all –
> Down to the stable,
> From heaven to earth;
> Follow the dream
> To see the birth.

> *The choir sings 'While Shepherds Watched'.
> (Words and music on page 162.)*

> *As the stars/angels leave, the shepherds (and any
> sheep) set off for Bethlehem. They move round
> the stage (through the audience if need be) and
> end up entering the stable area, sitting by Mary
> and Joseph. As the shepherds settle, three Kings
> appear, travelling. They come from the back of the
> hall and move through the audience if possible.*

Narrator:

> Three Kings came travelling to find the newborn
> baby.

Camel 1:   I was there. I saw it all.
We too were following the star.
The star that shone brighter than fire,

Camel 2:   I was there. I saw it all,
As we followed the star,
Brighter than a flame,
Brighter than the sun's eye.

Camel 3:   I was there. I saw it all,
As we travelled from far places –
The kings' faces fixed to the skies,
Eyes pinned on the star.

Narrator: First, they called at Herod's palace, thinking that a king would be born there.

Kings knock at imaginary palace door. Herod answers.

Kings 1, 2, 3 [*chant together*]:
We are travelling far,
following the star
that shines in the night.
We are following the light,
Sure that it shows the way
To the birth of the baby King.

Herod: Go to Bethlehem. That is where he is to be born. And when you have found him, come back and tell me. For I will want to visit him too . . .

Herod leaves.

King 1:   Mmmmm, not a nice piece of work.

King 2:   Up to no good, I'll be bound.

King 3:   Definitely not to be trusted!

Narrator: So it was that the three Kings set off again on their journey to Bethlehem. They followed the star. Each night it seemed to gleam brighter than ever. In the end, it led them not to a palace but to a poor stable.

They move round the stage and through the audience, ending up entering the stable area, before Mary and Joseph.

As they travel, the choir sings 'We Three Kings'. (Words and music on page 164.)

King 1:   I have brought Gold, fit for a King.

King 2:   I have brought Frankincense, fit for worship.

King 3:   I have brought Myrrh, a fragrant spice.

The Kings hand over their gifts, bow and take seats either side. There is a silence.

Mouse 1:   I was there. I saw it all.
Hidden in the straw
By the cattle stall.
I saw the beginning
Of the tale.

Narrator: And that is the end of our story.
We would like to wish you all a merry
Christmas and ask you to join us in singing.

Tumultuous applause as everyone sings 'We Wish You a Merry Christmas'. (Words and music on page 166.)

The angels and stars plus other characters come in and stand behind to the side of Mary and Joseph.

Little Donkey

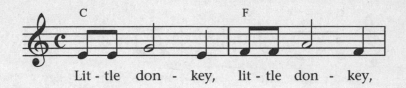

Lit - tle don - key, lit - tle don - key,

On the dus - ty road. Got to keep on

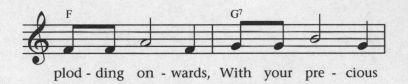

plod - ding on - wards, With your pre - cious

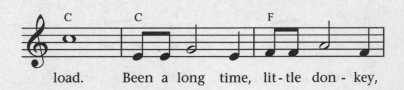

load. Been a long time, lit - tle don - key,

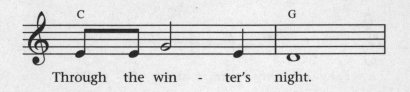

Through the win - ter's night.

Don't give up now, lit-tle don - key,

Beth - le- hem's in sight.

CHORUS

Ring out those bells to - night,

Beth - le - hem, Beth - le - hem.

Fol - low that star to - night,

There Isn't Any Room

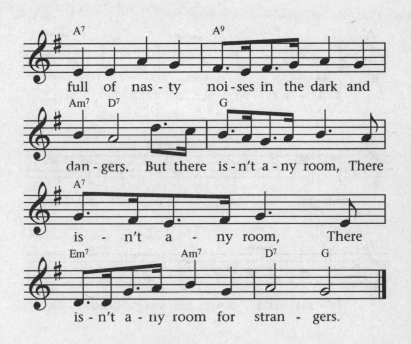

full of nas - ty noi - ses in the dark and

dan - gers. But there is - n't a - ny room, There

is - n't a - ny room, There

is - n't a - ny room for stran - gers.

2. Rat-a-tat-tat, Rat-a-tat-tat,
   Yes! Yes! Yes!
   There is a little room
   And you may stay here,
   We have a little place for strangers.
   Come in from the night
   To the stable so bare,
   Which is full of warmth and friendliness
       and safe from dangers.
   Yes, there is a little room,
   There is a little room,
   There is a little room for strangers.

Away in a Manger

1. A - way in a___ man - ger, no___ crib for a bed, The___ lit - tle Lord Je - sus laid___ down his sweet head. The stars in the___ bright sky looked down where he lay, The___ lit - tle Lord

Je - sus a - sleep on the hay.

2. The cattle are lowing, the Baby awakes,
   But little Lord Jesus, no crying he makes.
   I love thee, Lord Jesus, look down from the sky,
   And stay by my side until morning is nigh.

3. Be near me, Lord Jesus; I ask thee to stay
   Close by me for ever, and love me, I pray.
   Bless all the dear children in thy tender care,
   And fit us for heaven to live with thee there.

While Shepherds Watched

2. 'Fear not,' said he: for mighty dread
   Had seized their troubled mind;
   'Glad tidings of great joy I bring
   To you and all mankind.'

3. 'To you in David's town this day
   Is born of David's line
   A Saviour, who is Christ the Lord;
   And this shall be the sign:'

4. 'The heavenly Babe you there shall find
   To human view displayed,
   All meanly wrapped in swathing bands,
   And in a manger laid.'

5. Thus spake the seraph; and forthwith
   Appeared a shining throng
   Of angels praising God, who thus
   Addressed their joyful song:

6. 'All glory be to God on high,
   And to the earth be peace;
   Good will henceforth from heaven to men
   Begin and never cease.'

We Three Kings

1. We three kings of Or - i - ent are;

Bear - ing gifts we trav - erse a - far;

Field and foun - tain, moor and moun - tain,

Fol - low - ing yon - der star;

CHORUS

O____ star of won - der, star of night,

Star with roy - al beau - ty bright,

West - ward lead - ing still pro - ceed - ing,

Guide us to thy per - fect light.

2. *Melchior:*
Born a king on Bethlehem's plain,
Gold I bring, to crown him again –
King for ever, ceasing never,
Over us all to reign:
 O star of wonder, star of night,
 Star with royal beauty bright,
 Westward leading still proceeding,
 Guide us to thy perfect light.

We Wish You a Merry Christmas

1. We wish you a merry
Christ - mas, We wish you a mer - ry
Christ - mas, We wish you a mer - ry
Christ - mas, And a hap - py New Year.

CHORUS

Good ti - dings we bring To
you and your kin, We wish you a mer - ry

Christ - mas, And a hap - py New Year.

2. Now bring us some figgy pudding,
   Now bring us some figgy pudding,
   Now bring us some figgy pudding,
   And bring some out here.
       Good tidings we bring
       To you and your kin,
       We wish you a merry Christmas,
       And a happy New Year.

3. For we all like figgy pudding,
   For we all like figgy pudding,
   For we all like figgy pudding,
   So bring some out here.
       Good tidings we bring
       To you and your kin,
       We wish you a merry Christmas,
       And a happy New Year.

4. And we won't go until we've had some,
   And we won't go until we've had some,
   And we won't go until we've had some,
   So bring some out here.
       Good tidings we bring
       To you and your kin,
       We wish you a merry Christmas,
       And a happy New Year.

Persephone

by Julia Donaldson

This play is based on a Greek myth that
explains how winter came to exist.

Characters

In the Upper World
Demeter, the goddess of nature
Persephone, her daughter
Pearl ⎫
Coral ⎭ sea nymphs
Hecate, a very old goddess
Apollo, god of sun, music and poetry
Zeus, the king of the gods
Hera, Zeus's wife
Aphrodite ⎫
Athene ⎭ young beautiful goddesses
Hermes, the messenger of the gods
Alexis, a peasant boy
Alexis's mother
a miller
farmers 1, 2, 3 and 4
(Optional) additional non-speaking
   farmers and peasants

In the Underworld
Pluto, god of the underworld
Cerberus, Pluto's three-headed dog
Nicodemus, Pluto's page boy
servant 1
servant 2
servant 3 (Andros)
cook

OPENING CHORUS:

Demeter enters, followed by Alexis and his mother, the millers and the farmers, who carry fruit and corn. (Words and music on page 221.)

Demeter, Demeter,
She makes the apples sweeter,
And everywhere Demeter goes
The grass grows longer,
The plants grow stronger
And everything grows and grows.

Demeter, Demeter,
She makes the peaches sweeter,
And everywhere Demeter goes
The corn turns yellow,
The pears turn mellow
And everything grows and grows.

Persephone enters and takes Demeter's hand.

The sun shines on the water,
The rain falls on the land
When Demeter and her daughter
Go walking hand in hand.

Demeter, Demeter,
She makes the cherries sweeter,
And everywhere Demeter goes
The roots keep rooting,
The shoots keep shooting
And everything grows and grows.

The countryside looks jolly
In reds and pinks and greens
So it's goodbye melon-cauli,
We're feeling full of beans.

Demeter, Demeter,
She makes the apples sweeter,
And everywhere Demeter goes
The grass grows longer,
The plants grow stronger
And everything grows and grows.

The farmers etc. follow Demeter offstage.

SCENE 1:   **The Sea Nymphs**

A seashore by a meadow. Persephone and the two sea nymphs, Coral and Pearl, are playing tag on the beach.

Coral: Caught you, Pearl!

Pearl: Caught you, Coral!

Persephone [*in the meadow*]:
You can't catch me!

Coral: That's not fair, Persephone.

Pearl: You're supposed to stay on the beach!

Persephone: Why should I? I'm not a sea nymph.

Coral: No, but *we* are.

Pearl: We can't *live* away from the sea, remember!

Persephone [*coming back to the beach*]:
Oh, all right, but let's play something different.
Let's collect seaweed.

Demeter [*offstage*]:
Persephone! Persephone!

Coral: Your mother's calling you, Persephone.

Persephone: Oh no! Just when I'm enjoying myself. Now I'll
have to go and help her make things grow.

Pearl: That sounds like fun to me.

Persephone: Not when you have to do it every day.

Demeter [*entering*]:
        Persephone! I wish you wouldn't wander off.

Pearl: Good morning, Demeter. The flowers look lovely today. You must have been working hard.

Demeter: Thank you, Pearl – yes, I have.

Coral: Why don't you take the morning off?

Demeter [*laughing*]:
        No, Coral, I can't do that. I have to ripen all the apples today. Come on, Persephone.

Persephone: Oh, Mother, do I *have* to come?

Coral: Can't she stay here with us, Demeter?

Persephone: *Please*, Mother.

Demeter: I don't know, Persephone . . . if I let you, you must promise not to—

Persephone: I know, I know, not to talk to any strangers.

Demeter: And not to eat any food that anyone offers you.

Persephone: Oh, Mother, you do go on!

Pearl: We'll look after her, Demeter.

Demeter: I must say, I'd rather go on my own. Persephone usually eats half the fruit that we ripen.

Persephone: I can't help it, I *love* fruit. You'll bring me some apples back, won't you?

Demeter: Yes, Persephone, I will. Now, be good and don't wander off.

Persephone: No. Goodbye, Mother.

Exit Demeter.

Pearl: Look, here's some of that pretty kind of seaweed. You can have a necklace, Persephone! [*She drapes some seaweed round Persephone's neck.*] There, you look like one of us now!

Coral: I wish I could have a necklace of flowers.

Persephone: You can! I know where there are lots of flowers!

Pearl: But, Persephone, you're meant to stay with us.

Persephone: I won't go far!

Coral: She'll be fine! You sound just like Demeter, the way you go on.

Persephone [*wandering off*]:
                 See you soon!

Pearl: I hope she'll be all right.

Coral: Of course she will! Let's go for a swim till she comes back.

They run off.

SCENE 2: **The Capture**

A meadow. Enter Persephone, picking the petals off a daisy.

Persephone: Tinker, tailor, soldier, sailor, rich man, poor man, beggar man, thief – oh no, I'm going to marry a thief!

Enter Pluto with Servants 1 and 2.

Pluto: Good morning, Persephone. [*Persephone looks startled but says nothing.*] Well, don't you have a tongue in your head? Ah, I know, you've been told not to talk to strangers, is that it? But *I'm* not a stranger. I'm a great friend of your mother, the goddess Demeter, and *I'm* a god too. My servants will tell you which one.

Servant 1: He's Pluto.

Servant 2: The god of the Underworld.

Persephone backs away.

Pluto: Don't look so shocked, my dear. The Underworld is a very beautiful place.

Persephone: No it's not, it's a horrible, dark place. I've heard all about it.

Pluto: Now, now, you mustn't believe all the stories you hear.

Persephone: But there are no flowers there, and no grass!

Pluto: Maybe not, but we have jewels that are brighter than any flowers. Come and see, and I'll give you some to keep! Wouldn't you like a diamond necklace instead of this seaweed one?

Persephone: No!

Pluto: You'd love my pet as well.

Persephone: Pet? What pet?

Pluto: Cerberus, my three-headed dog. I can't wait to see his tail wagging when he sees the beautiful princess his master has brought back.

Persephone: You're not *going* to bring me back!

Pluto [*holding out his hand*]:
Persephone! I *beg* you to come with me.

Persephone: No! Go away!

Pluto: Now, now, Persephone, I don't want to have to force you. Take my hand.

Persephone: Help! [*She tries to run but the servants block her way.*]

Pluto: Seize her! [*The servants do so.*]

Persephone: Let go! Help! Pearl! Coral!

Servant 1: It's no use struggling.

Servant 2: You're coming with us.

Pluto: Hold her tight, but don't hurt her – remember she's going to be your queen.

Persephone: I'm *not*! Let me go!

Pluto: Take her to my carriage.

The servants go out with Persephone, who is screaming and struggling. She takes off her seaweed necklace and throws it to the ground. Pluto follows them out.

SCENE 3:   **Missing**

The seashore. Enter Coral and Pearl, who carries a shell bracelet.

Pearl: Persephone! Look what we've got! A bracelet of shells.

Coral [*snatching the bracelet*]:
Let *me* give it to her!

Pearl: That's not fair! I made it. [*Runs after Coral.*]

Enter Demeter with a basket of apples.

Coral: Oh, hello, Demeter. Mmm, what lovely-looking apples. Can I have one?

Demeter: Yes, of course, help yourselves. But where's Persephone?

Coral: Oh, she's around somewhere.

Demeter: What do you mean, 'around'? I can't see her.

Pearl: She's picking some flowers for us.

Demeter: What? You let her wander off?

Coral: We didn't want her to – it was her idea.

Pearl: You see, we made a seaweed necklace for her, and she wanted to make some flower ones for us.

Demeter: But I *told* you to stay with her. You promised!

Pearl: We tried to stop her.

Coral: We *couldn't* follow her. We die if we leave the seashore.

Demeter: Persephone! Persephone! Where has she got to?

Pearl: We'll search the beach, Demeter.

Demeter: And I'll look in the meadows. Persephone! Persephone!

They all wander off, calling her.

SCENE 4: **The First Clue**

Evening the same day. A meadow. Enter Alexis and his mother, who carries a basket of apples.

Alexis: These are the best apples I've ever tasted.

Mother: Don't eat any more or you'll make yourself sick.

Alexis: All right, I won't eat them, I'll juggle with them.

Mother: Stop that – look, you've dropped them, they'll be all bruised now.

Alexis [*picking up his apples, sees Persephone's seaweed necklace*]:
Look, what's this?

Mother: It's seaweed – that's strange!

Enter Demeter.

Mother: My goodness, here comes the goddess Demeter. [*She curtsies.*] Greetings, Mother Nature. Alex, stop juggling and get down on your knees.

Demeter: No, no, let the boy play.

Mother: Why do you look so sad, madam?

Demeter: Because I have lost my daughter, Persephone. Have you seen her?

Mother: No, madam, I'm sorry.

Alexis: I think I might have *heard* her.

Mother: Don't be silly, Alex – he's always making up stories.

Alexis: It's *not* a story.

Demeter: Let the child speak.

Alexis: Well, when I was climbing an apple tree I thought I heard someone calling for help . . . and there was another sound too.

Demeter: What was that?

Alexis: A sort of rattling, rumbling noise – like a carriage.

Mother: Probably just thunder.

Demeter: What's that you're carrying, child?

Alexis: It's some seaweed I found.

Demeter: Persephone's seaweed necklace! So she *has* been here. Persephone! Persephone!

Demeter goes off.

Mother: Poor woman!

Alexis: I thought you said she was a goddess.

Mother: She is, but she's a mother too, just like me. Look at the grass she's been walking on – it's all brown and withered.

Alexis [*biting an apple*]:
　　　　This apple tastes sour!

Mother:　　It must be because Demeter is unhappy.

　　　　They go off.

SCENE 5:　**Hecate**

　　　　A hillside, with the entrance to a cave. It is growing dark. Enter Demeter with a torch.

Demeter:　　Persephone! Where are you? Perhaps she's hiding in this cave. Persephone!

Hecate [*coming out of the cave*]:
　　　　Do I look like Persephone? She's a young girl and I, Hecate, am an old crone. Oh woe! Oh misery!

Demeter:　　What's the matter?

Hecate:　　Don't ask me that! Can't I make moan without everyone asking me what the matter is? Oh woe! Oh despair! Oh tearing out of hair!

Demeter:　　Can't you control yourself a bit? I'm not tearing out my hair and I really do have something to feel miserable about.

Hecate: Oh good! Then we can make moan together. Alas, alackaday!

Demeter: It's not day, it's night.

Hecate: So it is. All right then, alas, alackanight! Well, aren't you going to join in?

Demeter: No, I'm too busy looking for my daughter. Persephone!

Hecate: You'll never find her. She's probably been eaten by a dragon. Why don't you come into my cave and we can wail together till you are a withered old hag like me!

Demeter: No – I've vowed to take no rest, day or night. I've lit this torch from the fire of the volcano, and it will never go out till Persephone returns.

Hecate: In that case, let me go with you, and we can make moan together on the way.

Demeter: If you insist. Persephone! Persephone!

Hecate: Oh woe! Oh blackest of black beetles!

They go off together.

SCENE 6:   **The Underworld**

The Underworld. There is a table and a throne. Andros is setting the table with a plate, knife, fork, spoon, glass and jug. The cook hovers around fussily.

Cook: Is that table set, Andros?

Andros: Nearly.

Cook: Hurry up with the food, Nicodemus!

Enter Nicodemus with a trolley. On it are three plates of food. A loud barking is heard offstage.

Nicodemus: That's Cerberus barking! Pluto must be back.

Enter Pluto with Persephone, with Servants 1 and 2 and Cerberus. Everyone else bows. Cerberus leaps around barking.

Pluto: Down, Cerberus! Sit! Well, Persephone, what do you think so far? Do you like my Underworld palace?

Persephone: Not much.

Pluto: What? Didn't you notice all the golden statues?

And look, this is your throne – it's covered in emeralds!

Persephone: I don't *want* a throne – I'd rather sit on the grass. I want to go home!

Pluto: Perhaps you don't care for emeralds. But just wait till you see our diamonds. Tell her about them, everyone!

Pluto and the other underworld characters sing, to the tune of 'Charlie Is My Darling', 'The Underworld Song'. (Words and music on page 224.)

Our diamonds are enormous,
Enormous, enormous,
Our diamonds are enormous,
Oh yes, they are.
They're big and bright and beautiful,
They're quite spec-tac-u-lar.
You really ought to see them.

Persephone: I'd rather see a star.

Pluto and co.: Our diamonds are enormous
But she'd rather see a star.

Pluto [*spoken*]:
Perhaps she likes sapphires better than diamonds.

186

Pluto and co.:

> Our sapphires are stupendous,
> Stupendous, stupendous,
> Our sapphires are stupendous,
> Oh me, oh my!
> They must be even bluer than
> The twinkle in your eye.
> You really ought to see them.

Persephone: I'd rather see the sky.

Pluto and co.:

> Our sapphires are stupendous
> But she'd rather see the sky.

Pluto [spoken]:

> See if you can cheer her up, Cerberus.

> *Cerberus jumps up and tries to lick Persephone,*
> *who pushes him away.*

Pluto and co.:

> Our Cerberus has three heads,
> Yes, three heads, yes three heads.
> Our Cerberus has three heads,
> Upon my word!
> And each of them barks louder far
> Than any dog you've heard.
> You really ought to hear him.

Cerberus [*Vaguely to the same tune*]:
    Woof woof woof woof woof woof woof.

Persephone: I'd rather hear a bird.

Pluto and co.:
    Our Cerberus has three heads
    But she'd rather hear a bird.

Cerberus [*angry and disappointed*]:
    Woof woof woof woof!

Persephone: Take me home, Pluto. I hate it here.

Pluto: Come now, Persephone, I'm sure you'll see things differently when you've got a good meal inside you. Cook!

Cook: Yes, Your Majesty.

Pluto: What is the first course?

Cook: Curried snakes' eggs, Your Majesty.

Pluto: Ah, my favourite.

Persephone: I don't want any.

Pluto: Take it away!

Cook:	But, Your Majesty!
Pluto:	You heard what I said. Her ladyship wants to skip the starter. What have we next?
Cook:	Cockroaches in coal dust, Your Majesty.
Pluto:	I really can recommend this!
Persephone:	No! Please! Take it away.
Pluto:	How about something nice and sweet and sticky? What is the dessert, cook?
Cook:	Jellied worms with liquorice sauce, Your Majesty.
Persephone:	That looks disgusting!
Pluto:	What would you like then, my dear?
Persephone:	I just want to go home to my mother. [*She starts to cry.*]
Pluto:	Ah now, I think I *might* be able to help with that.
Persephone:	What? You'll take me back, you mean?

Pluto: Not exactly . . . Pour your mistress out a glass of Lethe water.

Cook: Yes, Your Majesty.

Persephone: What's this?

Pluto: It's some special water from one of my underground rivers. One sip of it will make you forget your mother and the world above. Then you can be happy here with me.

Persephone: No! I'd rather be sad and remember my mother than be happy and forget her!

Pluto: Very well, my dear, I won't force you. Come, I'll take you on a guided tour – I expect you'll feel hungrier after that. And if not, there's always tomorrow . . .

He leads Persephone out. Servants 1 and 2 follow. The cook, Nicodemus and Andros are left to clear away the rejected food, hampered by Cerberus who bounds about, trying to eat it.

SCENE 7: **Apollo**

The following morning. Enter Apollo. He sings (or recites) 'The Sun, the Sun, the Sun'. (Words and music on page 228.)

190

Apollo: Who turns the night into day?
The sun, the sun, the sun!
Who turns the grass into hay?
The sun, the sun, the sun!
Who in heaven do you suppose
Melts all the dewdrops on the rose,
Paints all the freckles on your nose?
The sun, the sun, the sun!
And you're never going to see
Anyone hotter than me.
I'm the sun, the sun, the one and only
Wonderful, wonderful sun!

Enter Demeter and Hecate.

Demeter: It's Apollo, the sun god.

Hecate: Oh horrible brightness! Oh hideous light!

Apollo: Good morning, ladies, what can I do for you?
Would you like a suntan or a few freckles, or
have you just come to admire me?

Demeter: No, Apollo, I have come to seek news of my
daughter, Persephone.

Hecate: I keep *telling* you, she's probably fallen off a
cliff.

Demeter: Do be quiet, Hecate. Apollo, you see everything that happens by day. Tell me, what has happened to Persephone?

Hecate: She's been pecked by vultures.

Apollo: No such thing.

Demeter: So you *have* seen her! Is she alive?

Apollo: Certainly, madam, and doing very well for herself. Congratulations.

Demeter: What do you mean?

Apollo: Your daughter is seated on a throne beside the ruler of the Underworld.

Demeter: Pluto!

Hecate: I knew it!

Apollo: An excellent match. Allow me to congratulate you in verse.
           Oh what a conquest! Oh what a catch!
           Oh what a fortunate, fabulous match!
           Oh what a triumph! Oh what—

Demeter: Do stop making up poetry and tell me what *happened* exactly.

Apollo: Your daughter was picking flowers in the meadow . . .
Pretty maiden
Making posies,
Picking poppies,
Plucking roses . . .

Demeter: GET ON WITH IT!

Apollo: Pluto spotted her and . . . er, whisked her off to the Underworld.

Demeter: In other words, he's *stolen* her. We'll see what the king of the gods has to say about that! Come, Hecate, let's go and complain to Zeus.

Apollo: I wouldn't do that, madam. There's little use in seeking Zeus . . . that was a good rhyme! Use/Zeus – I must remember that.

Demeter: Stop rambling! *Why* can't I get Zeus to rescue Persephone?

Apollo: Because he *wants* her to stay in the Underworld.

Demeter: How could he?

Apollo: Well, you know Pluto has been looking for an Underworld queen for some time.

Demeter: No.

Apollo: Oh yes. He's been making a terrible nuisance of himself, pestering all the goddesses. They kept complaining to Zeus about it. So when Zeus heard that Pluto had settled down at last, he was delighted.

Demeter: This is terrible!

Hecate: Oh wringing of hands! Oh gnashing of teeth! Come, Demeter, let's go back to my cave and tear out our hair together.

Demeter: No! If Zeus won't help me, I'll have to rescue Persephone myself.

Apollo: Demeter, don't talk nonsense. You'll never find the entrance to the Underworld. In any case, it's guarded by Pluto's three-headed dog, Cerberus.

Demeter: I'd tackle a *thirty*-headed dog to get my daughter back. Come on, Hecate, let's go.

Hecate: I'm sorry, Demeter, I can't take any more of your hope and determination. I'm going back to my cave. You can join me there as soon as you give up.

Demeter: That will be never!

Hecate and Demeter go their separate ways during Apollo's speech.

Apollo: Poor woman! What sorrow! What bravery! I think I'll make up a poem about it:
She roams through the land,
Her torch in her hand,
Seeking her daughter
Through fire and through water,
Her tears making streaks
On her lily-white cheeks . . .
Oh dear! I'm making myself cry. What about you, ladies? Ladies? They've gone!

He shrugs and saunters away.

SCENE 8: **Starvation**

Two people bring on a sign saying 'Six months later'.

Enter Alexis and his mother, looking cold, tired and hungry. The miller enters from the other direction.

Alexis: I'm cold.

Mother: I know you are, Alexis – everyone is.

Alexis: And I'm hungry too. Why is there no fruit on the trees?

Mother: We must make do without fruit. Look, here comes the miller – maybe he can let us have a little flour to make bread with. Good morning, miller.

Alexis: I'm not a miller any more. All the wheat in my barn is used up.

Alexis: Why don't you get some more?

Miller: I can't. No more will grow.

Mother: Look at the ground, it's frozen solid.

             Enter Demeter, followed by a group of farmers.

Farmers: Help us, Demeter. We're starving. Can you do something?

Mother [*down on her knees*]:
             Yes, Mother Demeter, help us! You're the only one who can!

Demeter: What is it you want?

Farmer 1: We want the plants to grow again!

Alexis: We want fruit on the trees!

Miller: I need wheat to make into flour.

Farmer 2: My chickens want corn.

Farmer 3: My cows will die without any grass to eat.

Farmer 4: We'll *all* die!

All: Help us, Mother Nature!

Demeter: I *can't* help you.

Alexis: Yes you can! I know you can. Remember all those juicy apples you used to fill the trees with!

Demeter: *Used* to, child, but not any more. Not since Pluto stole my daughter away. I've given up my other work while I search for her.

Miller: Isn't that a bit hard on us?

Demeter: I *couldn't* help you even if I tried. I'm so unhappy I've lost my power to make things grow.

Alexis: *I'll* help you get Persephone back! I'll fight Pluto.

Demeter:	It's no good. Zeus, the king of the gods, is on his side. He wants Persephone to stay in the Underworld.
Mother:	What? And for the grass to dry?
Miller:	And the corn to shrivel?
Farmer 1:	And the fruit to wither?
Farmer 2:	And the animals to starve?
Farmer 3:	And people to freeze?
Farmer 4:	And all of us to die?
Demeter:	It's no use complaining to *me*. Why don't you pray to Zeus instead?
Miller:	Yes, we'll do that. Zeus!
All:	Zeus! Zeus!
	Bring back the grass!
	Bring back the corn!
	Bring back the flowers!
	Bring back the fruit!
	Bring back the spring!
	Bring back the summer!
	BRING BACK PERSEPHONE!

> *The chant grows louder and louder. They repeat it as they march off.*

SCENE 9:   **Hide and Seek**

> *In the Underworld. Persephone, laughing, runs onstage and hides behind the curtains. Nicodemus, also laughing, runs on, looking for her. (They are playing hide and seek.)*

Nicodemus: Persephone! I know you're here!

Persephone [*jumping out*]:
Boo!

> *They both laugh.*

> *Pluto enters, carrying some Lethe water.*

Nicodemus: Oh, sorry, Your Majesty, we were just . . .

Pluto: Playing hide and seek, I know. It's good to hear you laugh, Persephone. I do believe you've come to like the Underworld just a little bit.

Persephone: The caves and twisty passages are good for hide and seek – but I'd still rather be in the open air.

Pluto: But just one sip of Lethe water could change that!

Persephone: No, Pluto, I'll never drink that. I don't want to forget my mother.

Pluto: Then if you'd only eat something. Just a tiny slice of spicy roast mole, perhaps? Or a nice crunchy rock cake? I do so want you to be happy with me.

Persephone: I know you do, Pluto, and I *have* grown quite fond of you. But I don't even *like* your kind of food. If I was going to eat anything, it would be something fresh and simple.

Pluto: Such as?

Persephone: Such as a piece of my mother's fruit.

Pluto: Why didn't you say so before?

Persephone: I haven't said I'll eat it anyway – I promised my mother I wouldn't eat anything.

Pluto: I'm sure she wouldn't mind you eating some of *her* food. What a good idea. Nicodemus!

Nicodemus: Yes, Your Majesty.

Pluto: Go the upper world and pick me some fruit.

Nicodemus: Yes, Your Majesty. [*Exits.*]

Persephone: I won't eat it!

Pluto: I feel sure we can tempt you, Persephone. Now, how about a game of chess? You know how much you love the jewelled chess pieces.

Persephone: Will you set me free if I win?

Pluto [*laughing*]:
You don't give up, do you?

Persephone: No, I don't.

They go off together.

SCENE 10: **Mount Olympus**

Two people come on with a sign saying 'Mount Olympus, Home of the Gods'.

There is a table, with five goblets and some grapes on it. Zeus is holding a banquet. Seated at the table are his wife Hera, Apollo, Aphrodite and Athene.

Zeus: Some more nectar for you, Athene?

Athene: Thank you, Zeus, it's delicious.

201

Zeus: How about you, Aphrodite? Would you like a top-up?

Aphrodite: That would be divine.

Hera: Don't offer me any more, will you – I'm only your wife.

Zeus: Very well, my dear, I won't. Now then, who else – how about Demeter?

Hera: You *know* she never comes to our banquets.

Zeus: That's true – what's she up to these days?

Apollo: Looking for Persephone.

Zeus: Oh dear, not *still*? It's been six months. I thought she'd have cheered up by now.

Apollo: Alas, poor goddess, all forlorn,
Wand'ring through the fields of corn . . .

Hera: I hate to interrupt, Apollo, but there aren't any fields of corn any more.

Farmers [off]:
Bring back the grass!
Bring back the corn!

Zeus: Oh no, not that again! I can't stand it.

Aphrodite: Just try and ignore it.

Farmers: Bring back the flowers!
Bring back the fruit!

Zeus: I can feel one of my headaches coming on.

Athene: Why don't you shoot a thunderbolt at them?
That'll shut them up.

Zeus: I tried that the other day, and it didn't.

Farmers: Bring back the spring!
Bring back the summer!

Apollo: Would you like me to go and calm them down
with some nice poetry?

Hera: They don't want poetry, they want food.

Farmers: Bring back Persephone!

Hera: Why don't you bring her back, Zeus – then we'd
have a bit of peace.

Zeus: What do you other goddesses think?

Aphrodite: No, *don't* set her free – Pluto will just come pestering me.

Athene: Or me, more likely.

Aphrodite: You must be joking!

Hera: I can't see why he should fancy either of you.

Zeus: Stop that squabbling, my headache's bad enough as it is.

Farmers [*louder*]:
Bring back the grass!
Bring back the corn!
Bring back the flowers!
Bring back the fruit!
Bring back the spring!
Bring back the summer!
BRING BACK PERSEPHONE!

Zeus: It's no use, I'm going to have to give in. Where's my messenger? Hermes!

Hermes [*racing in*]:
At your command!

Zeus: Get those wings flapping, I want you to take a message to Pluto.

Hermes: I go, I go! [*He races out again.*]

Zeus: Come back, I haven't told you what the message is yet.

Hermes [*racing back*]:
      Sorry.

Zeus: Tell him you've come to take Persephone back to her mother.

Hermes: I go, I go! [*He races out again.*]

Zeus: Come *back*, I haven't finished!

Hermes [*racing back*]:
      Sorry!

Zeus: Where was I up to?

Hermes: Take Persephone's mother back to her.

Zeus: No, you idiot – take Persephone to her mother – *unless* she's had anything to eat in the Underworld.

Hermes: I go, I go! [*He races away, then comes back.*] I've come back.

Zeus: So I see. That was rather quick, wasn't it?

Hermes: Well, I haven't *been* yet. Er . . . do I have to?

Zeus: Yes, of course, why?

Hermes: Well, I have the feeling Pluto's not going to be happy about this. He might be angry with me.

Zeus: And *I* might hurl a thunderbolt at you if you don't hurry up and go.

Hermes: I go, I go! [*He races off.*]

Athene: Oh no, now Pluto'll be after me again!

Aphrodite: *Me*, you mean.

Hera: Shut up, you two.

Voices: Bring back Persephone!
Bring back Persephone!
BRING BACK PERSEPHONE!

Zeus [*who has been getting more and more frazzled*]:
All right, *all right*! I'm *bringing* her back!

The chanting continues and the gods leave, blocking their ears.

SCENE 11: Escape

> *In the Underworld, Pluto and Persephone are playing chess.*

Persephone: Checkmate!

Pluto: You've won again! You're too clever for me.

Persephone: So how about setting me free?

> *Cerberus is heard barking in the distance. Nicodemus enters, out of breath, carrying a dried-up pomegranate.*

Nicodemus: Your Majesty . . .

Pluto: Ah, you're back, Nicodemus. What have you brought? Rosy apples? Juicy pears?

Nicodemus: Er . . . no, Your Majesty.

Pluto: What then?

Nicodemus: Just . . . this! [*He holds out the pomegranate.*]

Pluto: What's that supposed to be?

Nicodemus: It's a pomegranate, Your Majesty.

Pluto: A pomegranate? Would you call that a pomegranate, Persephone?

Persephone: Well, it could have been one once, I suppose.

Pluto: You hear that! It could have been one once. And you could have been a sensible young man once, instead of a useless halfwit!

Nicodemus: But, Your Majesty, let me explain . . .

Pluto: Silence!

Persephone: Don't be mean, Pluto. Listen to what he has to say.

Pluto: Very well, just for you. But it had better be good.

Nicodemus: Well, Your Majesty, this was all I could find. All the trees were bare and the plants had died. I couldn't even find a blade of grass.

Pluto: What nonsense is this?

Nicodemus: It's true, Your Majesty. People are saying that Demeter is too sad to make anything grow.

Persephone: Oh no! My poor mother. Pluto, you *must* let me go back to her.

Cerberus is heard barking wildly.

Pluto: What's up with Cerberus? I'd better go and see. [*Exits.*]

Nicodemus: I'm sorry, Persephone, I really did try to find some nice fresh fruit.

Persephone: It's all right, Nicodemus. I wouldn't have eaten it anyway . . . though I do love pomegranates.

Nicodemus: I'm sorry this one's so dried up.

Persephone: It might not be so dry inside.

Nicodemus: I'll cut it open. [*He does so.*]

Persephone: Oh, I'd forgotten what fruit looked like. It reminds me so much of my mother!

Nicodemus: Won't you have just a little taste?

Persephone: Well, maybe just a nibble . . . while Pluto's not here. [*She takes a small bite.*] Mmm, I can almost see the upper world.

Enter Pluto and Hermes, with Cerberus gambolling around them.

Hermes: That's some dog you've got there, Pluto.

209

Pluto: Sorry about that, Hermes. Down, Cerberus. Are you all right?

Hermes: Yes, just about . . . Actually I'm more frightened of you than of Cerberus.

Pluto: Why, have you brought me bad news?

Hermes: I'm afraid so.

Pluto: Well, don't just stand there, tell me what Zeus has to say.

Hermes: He says you must . . . give Persephone back.

Persephone: Yes!

Pluto: No! Never! I don't believe it! You're making this up, Hermes. How *dare* you?

Hermes: I *knew* you'd be angry! It's not *my* fault, I'm just the messenger.

Pluto: So I'm to give up Persephone, just like that? Is there no way of avoiding it?

Hermes: Just a moment, there was something . . . what was it? Oh yes, that's it. You *can* keep Persephone here if she's had anything to eat while she's been with you.

Pluto: I see.

Persephone looks at Nicodemus and puts her finger to her lips.

Hermes: Well, has she?

Pluto: I can't lie. She's refused everything I've offered her.

Hermes [*turning to Persephone*]:
Then you're to come with me!

Persephone: When can we go?

Hermes: Straight away! [*He starts to charge out.*]

Persephone: Wait a second, I must say goodbye. [*Pluto has his back turned.*] Goodbye then, Pluto. Don't look so sad! Maybe I can come back and visit you . . .

Pluto: Who do you think you're fooling? Demeter will never let you out of her sight again.

Persephone: Well, goodbye anyway. All right then, Hermes, I'm ready.

Nicodemus: Aren't you going to say goodbye to *me*?

Persephone: Nicodemus, of course! How could I forget? I'll always remember our games of hide and seek.

Hermes: Do come on, Persephone, I'm getting itchy feet.

Persephone: All right, let's go!

Hermes takes her hand and they race out together.

Nicodemus: Shall I clear the table, Your Majesty?

Pluto: Yes. No, wait! Let me taste a morsel of the pomegranate first. It could make Persephone feel nearer.

Nicodemus: Yes, Your Majesty.

Pluto: What's this . . . it's already been cut open. Someone's eaten a bit. Was it you?

Nicodemus: No, Your Majesty.

Pluto: Who then? Speak! Was it Persephone? [*Nicodemus is silent.*] It *was*, wasn't it?

Nicodemus: She just had a mouthful, Your Majesty. She can't have eaten more than six seeds.

Pluto: This changes everything!

Nicodemus: Where are you going?

Pluto: After them, of course, and you're coming with me. Persephone has eaten in my kingdom. She's mine forever!

He goes out, pulling Nicodemus with him.

SCENE 12: The Judgement

The seashore. Demeter is wandering around, looking tired. Her torch has gone out but she has not noticed this. Enter Coral and Pearl.

Coral: Good morning, Demeter.

Pearl: Still no sign of Persephone?

Demeter: No.

Coral: Don't you ever rest?

Demeter: No. I will search and this torch will burn until Persephone returns.

Coral: But your torch *isn't* burning.

Demeter: How strange! It's gone out – can Zeus be playing tricks on me?

Pearl: Look, here's a daisy.

Demeter: That's impossible.

Coral: And another one.

Demeter: I don't understand this.

            Persephone runs onstage.

Persephone: Mother!

Demeter: Persephone! Am I dreaming?

Persephone: No, it's really me! Zeus sent Hermes to bring me back.

Hermes [*entering, laughing*]:
            It felt more like you bringing me! I could hardly keep up, even with the wings on my heels.

Persephone [*hugging Demeter*]:
            Oh, it's so good to see the grass again! Nicodemus said it had all died.

Hermes: It had, but everywhere you tread it's been springing back again.

Pearl: Persephone! We've missed you so much!

Coral: Was it terrible in the Underworld?

Persephone: It wasn't so bad once I got used to it. Pluto was very kind to me.

Demeter: Kind! How could you call him kind when he stole you away from me?

Persephone: But he was so lonely, Mother. I helped to cheer him up.

Coral: What does he look like? Is he very ugly?

Persephone: No, he's tall and proud-looking, and he always dresses in fine clothes and jewels.

Pluto [*entering, followed by Nicodemus*]:
            Just like this!

Persephone: Pluto!

Demeter: What are you doing here!

Pluto: I have come for Persephone.

Demeter: No! She belongs here!

Hermes: Remember Zeus's command, Pluto.

Pluto: Yes, I *do* remember Zeus's command. Persephone could return, provided she had eaten nothing.

Hermes: Well? You told me yourself she had refused everything you offered her.

Pluto: Everything except this! [*He holds out the pomegranate half.*]

Demeter: You're making this up, Pluto. I'm sure my daughter wouldn't want such a shrivelled-up pomegranate. Would you, Persephone?

Pluto: Well, Persephone?

Persephone: Nicodemus, you told him!

Nicodemus: I'm sorry, Persephone. I *meant* to keep it a secret, but I found I couldn't lie to Pluto, and . . . I wanted you back too.

Demeter: So it's true!

Persephone: It was only a little nibble. I'm sure it doesn't really count!

Pluto: Come with me, Persephone.

Demeter: No, she's staying here.

Zeus [*entering*]:
What are you trying to do – tear the poor girl in half?

Everyone: Zeus!

Zeus: Hermes, have you muddled up my message – it was only Persephone you were supposed to bring back from the Underworld, not Pluto as well.

Pluto: Persephone is mine! She has eaten with me, and now she must stay with me.

Demeter: But all she ate was six seeds of a pomegranate – one of *my* pomegranates!

Zeus: Persephone, is this true?

Persephone: Yes, it is.

Zeus: Very well. For every seed you ate you must spend one month of each year underground with Pluto.

Demeter: No! I can't part with Persephone again!

Zeus: Wait – but for the other six months she shall stay here with you.

Demeter: Am I to lose you for half of every year?

Persephone: Don't be so sad, Mother. I'll be glad to keep Pluto company.

Pluto: I'll look after her, Demeter.

Nicodemus: And she can play hide and seek with me.

Persephone: It won't be so bad next time – you'll know that I'll be coming back.

Demeter: Very well, Zeus. But when Persephone is away, the plants will die and the seeds will stay buried in the earth. We shall call it winter.

Pearl: Don't think of that time yet, Demeter – Persephone's six months on earth are only just beginning.

Persephone: We've got the whole summer to look forward to!

           Farmers, miller, Alexis and his mother and two Underworld servants enter with flowers, fruit and corn.

All: Demeter, Demeter,
           She makes the apples sweeter,
           And everywhere Demeter goes
           The grass grows longer,

The plants grow stronger
And everything grows and grows.

Enter Hecate, followed by remaining characters.

Hecate: Can't you turn the jollification down! I can't hear myself moan.

Demeter: Never mind your moaning, Hecate. Persephone's back. Come and celebrate with us.

Hecate: Oh all right, just this once, but I'll have to moan extra hard afterwards to make up for it.

All: Demeter, Demeter,
She makes the peaches sweeter,
And everywhere Demeter goes
The corn turns yellow,
The pears turn mellow
And everything grows and grows.

The sun shines on the water,
The rain falls on the land
When Demeter and her daughter
Go walking hand in hand.

Demeter, Demeter,
She makes the cherries sweeter,
And everywhere Demeter goes
The roots keep rooting,
The shoots keep shooting
And everything grows and grows.

The countryside looks jolly
In reds and pinks and greens
So it's goodbye melon-cauli,
We're feeling full of beans.

Demeter, Demeter,
She makes the apples sweeter,
And everywhere Demeter goes
The grass grows longer,
The plants grow stronger
And everything grows and grows.

Demeter, Demeter

1. De -

- - me - ter,___ De - me - ter,___ She
- - me - ter,___ De - me - ter,___ She
- - me - ter,___ De - me - ter,___ She
- - me - ter,___ De - me - ter,___ She

makes the ap - ples sweet - er,___ And
makes the pea - ches sweet - er,___ And
makes the cher - ries sweet - er,___ And
makes the ap - ples sweet - er,___ And

eve - ry - where De - me - ter
eve - ry - where De - me - ter
eve - ry - where De - me - ter
eve - ry - where De - me - ter

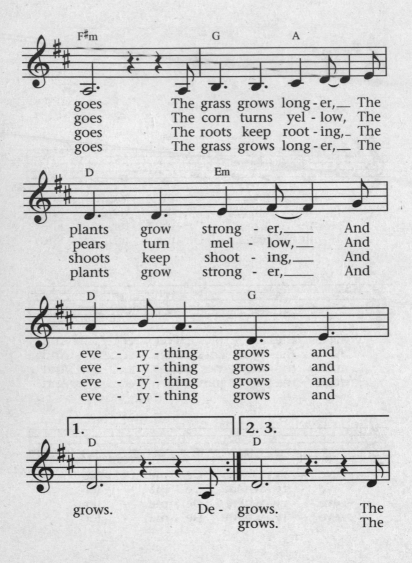

goes   The grass grows long - er,__ The
goes   The corn turns yel - low, The
goes   The roots keep root - ing,_ The
goes   The grass grows long - er,__ The

plants   grow   strong - er,____ And
pears   turn   mel - low,__ And
shoots   keep   shoot - ing,__ And
plants   grow   strong - er,____ And

eve - ry - thing   grows   and
eve - ry - thing   grows   and
eve - ry - thing   grows   and
eve - ry - thing   grows   and

grows.   De - grows.   The
                   grows.   The

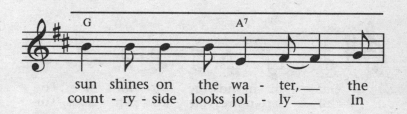

sun shines on the wa - ter,___ the
count - ry - side looks jol - ly___ In

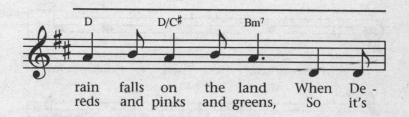

rain falls on the land When De -
reds and pinks and greens, So it's

-me - ter and her daugh - ter___ Go
good - bye me - lon - cau - li,___ We're

walk - ing hand in hand. De - grows.
feel - ing full of beans. De -

The Underworld Song

Our dia-monds are e - nor - mous, e -
Our sap-phires are stu - pen - dous, stu-

-nor - mous, e - nor - mous. Our
-pen - dous, stu - pen - dous. Our

dia - monds are e - nor - mous, Oh
sap - phires are stu - pen - dous, Oh

yes, they are. They're big and bright and
me, oh my! They must be e - ven

beau - ti - ful, They're quite spec - tac - u -
blu - er than the twin - kle in your

- lar.   You   real - ly ought to
eye.   You   real - ly ought to

see____ them._ I'd   ra - ther see   a
see____ them._ I'd   ra - ther see   the

star.   Our   dia - monds are   e -
sky.   Our   sap - phires are   stu -

- nor - mous but   she'd   ra - ther see   a
- pen - dous but   she'd   ra - ther see   the

star.   Our   Cer - ber - us   has
sky.

three heads, yes three heads, yes

three heads. Our Cer - ber - us has

three heads, up - on my word And

each of them barks loud - er far than

a - ny dog you've heard. You

real - ly ought to hear___ him. Woof

woof, woof woof, woof woof, woof woof_ I'd

ra - ther hear a bird. Our

Cer - ber - us has three heads but she'd

ra - ther hear a bird.

The Sun, the Sun, the Sun

Who turns the night in - to day? The
sun! The sun! The sun!
Who turns the grass in - to hay? The
sun! The sun! The sun!
Who in Hea - ven do you sup - pose
melts all the dew drops on the rose?

Finding a Baby
A Play for Christmas

by Fred Sedgwick

Characters

4 Angels
4 Shepherds
An Old Man
Bishop Nicholas (Father Christmas)
Lambs
A Woman
Children as Narrators
Kings or Queens
A Teacher (real one, or children acting him/her)

OVERTURE: (A single recorder plays a carol; or a piano, melody only. Probably 'Good King Wenceslas', but, as with everything in this play, this is flexible. The point is that the play starts very quietly, and grows and grows to a climax.) *Child 1 appears in front of the curtain, or at the front of an empty stage, dressed in his/her best (as are all the children).*

Child 1:   I was on my way to school today and I met some angels.

Enter Angels, one by one.

Angel 1 [like a newsreader, seriously, perhaps at a TV newsreader's desk]:
Here is the news from Bethlehem.

Angel 2 [less seriously]:
Glory to God in the highest [*From now on, the voices get more and more excited*]

Angel 3:   and peace on earth

Angel 4:   to all people of goodwill.

Angel 1:   For unto us

Angel 2:   a child is born

Angel 3:   A SON IS GIVEN

Angel 4:   and his name shall be called

                 [*From now on, shouted*]

Angel 1:   Wonderful! Counsellor!

Angel 2:   The mighty God!

Angel 3:   The Everlasting Father!

All Angels: The Prince of Peace!

                 [*Here there could be sounds of celebration
                 from the school orchestra.*]

                 *Angels wait, half on one side, half on the
                 other. Maybe Angel 1 goes to his news desk at
                 the side.*

                 Child 2 appears.

Child 2:   I was on my way to school today and I met
                 some angels – and some shepherds.

                 Four Shepherds enter.

Shepherd 1: We were frightened

Shepherd 2:	scared
Shepherd 3:	out of our wits
Shepherd 4:	but now [*he doesn't look it*] we are brave
Shepherd 1:	so let's go to Bethlehem
Shepherd 2:	to see this thing
Shepherd 3:	that has happened
Shepherd 4:	that the Lord has made known to us.

The Shepherds wait, some on one side, some on the other.

Child 3 appears.

Child 3: I was on my way to school today and I met some angels, some shepherds and some lambs, and a donkey.

Lots of animal noises, soft toys displayed by anybody around. Or children dressed as animals. The school orchestra might have prepared a range of animal sounds, including birds.

Child 4 appears.

235

Child 4:   I was on my way to school today and I met some angels, some shepherds and some lambs, a donkey and a few kings and queens.

King/Queen 1: I saw a star, and I'm looking for a baby.

King/Queen 2: It's been a long journey. Rotten time of year for a journey. Sometimes I wished I'd stayed at home. But I've got a present – and I'm not telling you what it is till Christmas Day.

All Children: Go on! Tell us what it is!

King/Queen 2: Certainly not! You'll have to wait till Christmas morning!

Children groan.

King/Queen 3: I've got a present. And it's myrrh.

Child 4: [*knowing look to audience*]:
       And they want us to do this myrrh often!

King/Queen 4: and there's gold, for a king. And frankincense.

Child 5 appears.

Child 5:   I was on my way to school today and I met some angels, some shepherds and some lambs, a donkey, a few kings and queens – and an old man.

Old Man enters.

Old Man: I wrote a poem once. Want to hear it?

Audience: [*Silence, probably*]

Children: We'd like to hear it. We like poetry!

Old Man: I'm going to say it anyway.

Overture music, same carol, this time with more than just a single instrument. Piano added? Or recorder. As Old Man begins, music dies away.

Old Man: I wrote a poem.
A little kid
Chalked this poem
On a dustbin lid.

The poem grew
And it grew and grew –
It was bigger than me
And bigger than you.

It was bigger than Miss
As it unfurled.
It was bigger than everything,
Even the world.

It was bigger than the sea
And the sky above
It was bigger than the universe

[*Long pause here*]

And its name was love.

Child 6 enters.

Child 6:   I was on my way to school today and I met some angels, some shepherds, some lambs, a donkey, a few kings and queens, an old man and a woman.

Woman enters.
[*The woman could be played by a real teacher.*]
Remaining Children enter.

Woman: Once there was a family. The mother had been dead many years. The father was out of work. They had little food. Scaps of bread, old vegetables, bony fatty meat. Often the children had to go into the centre of town to beg. Some people gave them food. Some didn't.

Child 7:	One night in winter, the food ran out.
Woman:	The cupboard was more bare than Mother Hubbard's, more bare than a desert.
Child 8:	No chicken, no beef,
Child 9:	no veg, no leaf,
Child 10:	nothing to put between their lips,
Child 11:	no pizza, curry, fish and chips.
Child 7:	But Bishop Nicholas, an important man in the city, heard about them.
Child 11:	Bishop Nicholas?
Child 12:	Yeah! Santa Claus!
All Children:	Father Christmas!
Child 7:	And he thought, why should anyone be so poor they can't get enough to eat?
Woman:	Good point.
Child 7:	And he filled a sack with toys
Child 1:	and turkey and wine and fruit and vegetables –

Child 7:	what about chocolate?
Child 1:	and chocolate
Child 2:	and he found the poor man's house
Child 3:	under the sign of the big star
Child 4:	and tipped it down the chimney!

Bishop enters.

Everyone cheers as Bishop Nicholas/Father Christmas tips a load of goodies on the stage. Here he can do whatever he fancies – move around the audience, make people laugh, etc. etc.

Carol: 'Good King Wenceslas', with more instruments.

Enter Teacher.

Teacher:	I met a child who was looking for a baby.
Child 5:	I was on my way to school today and I met some angels, some shepherds, some lambs, a donkey, a few kings and queens, an old man, a woman, my teacher (hello, Miss!) [*pause*] but I was really [*pause*] really [*pause*] really [*pause*] looking for a baby.

240

The traditional scene is suddenly exposed.

Child 6:   And there he is!

Child 7:   And they all sat down

             They sit down.

Child 8:   And there were Mary and Joseph and Jesus.

Child 9:   Look! Some angels, shepherds, some lambs, a donkey, a few kings and queens, an old man, a woman, my teacher.

Child 10:   And Father Christmas!

Child 11:   And they've found a baby!

             Final carol, with as much instrumentation as possible, in contrast to Overture. Everyone singing, including audience if possible. Crescendo to a rousing conclusion.

             After the carol, stage clears until only Angel 1 is left, tidying his or her papers, as newsreaders do.

             Pause.

Angel 1:   And that was the news from Bethlehem today.

The Little Eagle

by Vanessa Vian

We all know the story of the ugly duckling.
This play tells a very different story . . . a story where looking different doesn't matter and where everyone works together even though they may not all look the same.

Characters

Narrator 1	Father Eagle
Narrator 2	Mother Eagle
Narrator 3	Baby Eagle 1
Narrator 4	Baby Eagle 2
Narrator 5	
Mother Chicken	
Little Eagle	
Child 1	
Child 2	
Child 3	
Child 4	
Child 5	
Mother	
Father	
Chicken 1	
Chicken 2	
Chicken 3	
Chicken 4	
Chicken 5	
Chicken 6	
Chicken 7	
Postman	
Chick 1	
Chick 2	
Chick 3	
Chick 4	

Narrator 1:	Once there was a tall mountain – so tall that its top touched the silence of the clouds.
Narrator 2:	At the very top of this mountain two eagles had built their nest and, safe and warm in the centre of this nest, lay three eggs.
Narrator 3:	One night a tremendous storm lashed the mountaintop. The wind was so strong that one of the eggs was blown right out of the nest and down the mountainside. Finally it landed in the soft grass of a field at the foot of the mountain.
Narrator 4:	The next morning the clouds had been blown from the sky and the sun shone brightly. Five children from the farm near by were out playing.
	Group of 5 Children enter and go to centre of stage.
Child 1:	I hope no trees have blown over.
Child 2:	I'm glad we were safe in bed.
Child 3:	Come on – let's play.

Child 4:	Hey! Come and look at this! I've found a great big egg! [*Picks up egg and holds it up for the others to see.*]
Child 5:	Wow, it's enormous! Let me hold it.
Child 4:	No. I found it.
Child 1:	I'll look after it – you two will break it. We'll take it home to show Mum and Dad.
	Children walk round stage – Mother and Father come on to stage – children meet up with Mother and Father.
Child 2:	Mum! Dad! Look what we've found!
Child 3:	Where do you think it came from?
Child 4:	What shall we do with it?
Mother:	What a large egg! It must have fallen from a nest in last night's storm.
Father:	Let's put it with the chickens. They may be able to hatch it out.

*Children, Mother and Father go off. Chickens
enter on right side of stage. Father enters with
egg – leaves children on the floor by the stage,
watching him.*

Father: Quietly now. [*Puts finger to lips, then goes
over to Mother Chicken and places egg by
her. Father strokes her.*]

Father: There . . . let's put this with your eggs.

Family go off.

Narrator 5:   When the mother chicken's eggs hatched, she
was pleased to see . . . one yellow fluffy chick.

Chick 1 enters and goes to centre of stage.

Narrator 5:   two yellow fluffy chicks . . .

Chick 2 enters and stands next to Chick 1.

Narrator 5:   three yellow fluffy chicks . . .

Chick 3 enters and stands next to Chick 2.

Narrator 5:   four yellow fluffy chicks . . .

Chick 4 enters and stands next to Chick 3.

Narrator 5:   AND . . .

Little Eagle enters and stands next to Chick 4.

Narrator 5:   one chick that was not at all yellow or fluffy.

Mother Chicken leaves chicken group and walks along the front of the line of chicks from Chick 1 end, looking at each one in turn and straightening their feathers.

Mother Chicken:

Well . . . aren't you all beautiful!

Comes to Little Eagle and stops.

Mmm . . . you DO look very different from the others. Never mind. I think you are just as lovely as them. Off you all go and play together.

Mother Chicken rejoins the chicken group, leaving Chicks in a semicircle around Little Eagle.

Chick 1:   You are a very big chick.

Chick 2:   Your beak looks VERY sharp.

Chick 3:   Your wings look MUCH stronger than ours.

Chick 4:   Come on. You'll be good at all the games.

                 Chicks put their wings round Little Eagle and lead him to right edge of stage. Chicks go off – Little Eagle turns and comes back to Mother Chicken.

Little Eagle: Mother, I don't look like the other chicks. What am I?

Mother Chicken:

                 I was wondering that. I know, let's ask the others. Excuse me – could you all help?

                 Mother Chicken calls over the group of Chickens. Chickens come down from right side of stage and form a large semicircle around Little Eagle, looking at him and pretending to discuss him with each other.

Mother Chicken:

                 Do any of you know what sort of bird my chick is?

Chicken 1:   Large strong feathers.

Chicken 2:   A VERY large beak.

Chicken 3:   Long, powerful wings – he's certainly going to be good at flying.

Chicken 4:   Sharp talons.

Chicken 5:   Round, golden eyes.

Chicken 6:   Strong legs.

Chickens all turn to each other to discuss.

Chicken 7:   Yes. We are all agreed.

Mother Chicken:
Well?

Chicken 7:   He's definitely [*long pause*] not a chicken!

All chickens return to right side of stage, still discussing amongst themselves.

Little Eagle: Oh dear. If I'm not a chicken will I have to leave?

Mother Chicken:
Don't be silly. It doesn't matter two clucks what you look like or where you came from. I'm looking after you. Whatever happens, always remember – I love you.

Postman calls from offstage.

Postman: Delivery for Mrs Chicken. Delivery for Mrs Chicken.

Postman enters and gives Mother Chicken the delivery.

Postman: Here's the 'What's That Bird?' book that you ordered.

Mother Chicken: Oh, thank you.

Postman leaves. Mother Chicken talks to Little Eagle.

Mother Chicken: Come on. We'll look together and find out what you are.

They sit down together on left side of stage and look through book.

Little Eagle: There! That's me. What does it say?

Mother Chicken: It says 'EAGLE'. Isn't that exciting! I've never had an eagle in the family before. Well, I'm going to help you to be the best eagle you can possibly be.

Mother Chicken stays seated. Little Eagle stands up and goes to centre of stage.

Narrator 1: That night, when most of the chickens were asleep, the little eagle stood outside, looking up at the stars.

Chicken 3: Come on, lad. You should be inside. What are you looking at?

Little Eagle: The stars. They are so beautiful. I wish I knew more about them.

Chicken 7: Chickens don't look up at stars. We're not interested in them. We make sure we are inside when it is dark.

Mother Chicken comes over.

Mother Chicken:
Ah, there you are. Time for bed.

Little Eagle: Look up. Aren't they beautiful?

Mother Chicken:
I don't know about stars, but I can help you find out.

Postman calls from offstage.

Postman:	Delivery for Mrs Chicken. Delivery for Mrs Chicken.

Postman enters and gives Mother Chicken the delivery.

Postman:	Here's the 'Name That Star' book you ordered.

Mother Chicken:	Oh, thank you.

Postman leaves. Mother Chicken turns to speak to Little Eagle.

Mother Chicken:	Come on. Let's learn together.

Narrator 2:	And the little eagle sat with his mother under the stars.

Little Eagle goes to sleep with Mother Chicken's wing around him. She gently strokes his head.

Narrator 3:	The next morning the young eagle was up early.

Little Eagle goes to centre of stage.

Narrator 4:	He was looking up at the sky again – not at the stars this time but at the high clouds.

Chickens 4, 5 and 6 come over to join Little Eagle.

Chicken 5:	Let's look for some seeds to eat.
Chicken 6:	Come on, lad. You won't find any up there.
Little Eagle:	Look up. Imagine what it would be like to fly with the clouds.
Chicken 4:	Chickens don't do much flying. We're not interested in it.

Chickens 4, 5 and 6 return to right side of stage – Mother Chicken comes over to Little Eagle.

Mother Chicken:

Well, if you want to fly, I'll help you.

Postman calls from offstage.

Postman:	Delivery for Mrs Chicken. Delivery for Mrs Chicken.

Postman enters and gives Mother Chicken the delivery.

Postman: Here's your 'How to Fly in Five Easy Lessons'. Good luck!

Mother Chicken:
Thank you.

Postman leaves. Mother Chicken turns to Little Eagle.

Mother Chicken:
Now, if we work hard together, I'm sure we'll have you up there, flying, in no time.

Narrator 5: And his mother took the little eagle to the highest part of the farm and there they began his flying lessons.

Mother Chicken and Little Eagle go to left side of stage where they work on his flying. Mother Eagle and Father Eagle enter with two young eagles between them. Slow, solemn music for them to 'fly' in time with. They 'fly' in front of stage and then enter stage from the left.

Father Eagle: This is the only place that we haven't looked.

Mother Eagle: If he's not here, we will have to go back to the mountain.

All the eagles begin to look around.
Mother Chicken brings Little Eagle across
from the left side of stage – they have not seen
the eagle family yet.

Mother Chicken:

That was excellent. You had both feet right
off the ground. Tomorrow is Christmas Day.
We could practise again in the afternoon.

Baby Eagle 1: Look, over there!
[*Points to Little Eagle.*]

Baby Eagle 2: He looks just like us.

Mother Eagle: We've found him!

Mother Eagle goes up to Little Eagle and
hugs him.

Father Eagle: Leave these chickens and come with us . . .
back to our mountain.

Little Eagle [*turns to Mother Chicken*]:
Oh . . . may I go?

Mother Chicken:

If that is what you want.

Little Eagle: Goodbye!

256

Little Eagle joins eagle family and flies off with them. All eagles leave stage. Mother Chicken watches him go and, as he disappears from view, she waves and calls to him, sadly.

Mother Chicken:
Goodbye.

Narrator 1: And the little eagle flew off, back to the mountain, leaving his mother sad and alone.

Narrator 2: Mother Chicken picked up the Christmas present that she had made for the little eagle.

Narrator 3: I didn't even have time to give him this, she thought sadly.

Mother Chicken puts a hankie up to her eye – looks up at the sky and then looks down at the Christmas present (a scarf) that she had made for Little Eagle.
Little Eagle enters without Mother Chicken seeing him. He walks over to her and touches her gently on her shoulder. She turns and sees him and smiles at him.

Little Eagle: I'm back!

Mother Chicken:
> Oh, I thought you'd gone back to the mountain.

Little Eagle:
> Oh no. I couldn't leave you. The eagles have said that I can fly with them whenever I like. But I shall always come back here. This is my home and you are my mother.

Mother Chicken:
> Thank you. I think I'd better give this to you now. [*Places scarf around Little Eagle's neck.*] It's to keep you warm when you fly with the clouds.

Little Eagle:
> Thank you. It's lovely. This is for you. [*Gives Mother Chicken a toy eagle.*] It's ME! It's so you remember me when I am away, flying.

Mother Chicken:
> He's beautiful. [*Looks up at Little Eagle.*] In fact, he's the best eagle I've ever known.

Narrator 4:
> And the little eagle lived happily with his mother. He soared with the eagles whenever he wanted, but he ALWAYS returned home. And that is the end of the story of the little eagle.

Christmas Jokes

SHANE: How are you getting on with the guitar your dad gave you for Christmas?
WAYNE: Oh, I threw it away.
SHANE: Why did you do that?
WAYNE: It had a hole in the middle.

What's the best Christmas present?
Difficult to say, but a drum takes a lot of beating.

What do Santa's elves say when they get back to Lapland after delivering the presents on Christmas Eve?
'Gnome, sweet gnome.'

What's the wettest animal in the world?
A reindeer.

Why is it hard to keep a secret at the North Pole?
Because your teeth chatter.

FIRST BOY: Where does you mum come from?
SECOND BOY: Alaska.
FIRST BOY: Don't worry, I'll ask her myself.

What's white and flies upwards?
A silly snowflake.

FIRST SPIDER: What shall I buy my husband for Christmas?
SECOND SPIDER: Buy him what I bought mine – four pairs of socks.

What did the Christmas stocking say when it had a hole in it?
'Well, I'll be darned!'

What sort of sheet can't be folded?
A sheet of ice.

What often falls at the North Pole but never gets hurt?
Snow.

What's Santa's wife called?
Mary Christmas.

DAD: Would you like a pocket calculator for Christmas?
DENNIS: No, thanks, I already know how many pockets I've got.

What can you give a deaf fisherman for Christmas?
A herring aid.

What do sad Christmas trees do?
They pine a lot.

What do gorillas sing at Christmas?
'Jungle bells, jungle bells . . .'

Why does Santa climb down chimneys?
Because it soots him.

BEN: Did you like the dictionary I gave you for Christmas?
LEN: Yes, I've been trying to find the words to thank you.

What do you call a little lobster who won't share his
Christmas presents?
Shellfish.

Knock, knock.
Who's there?
Harvey.
Harvey who?
Harvey going to open our presents yet?

What's red and white, bounces, and goes 'Ho, ho, ho'?
Santa on a pogo stick.

MARY: I'm giving my dad banana skins for Christmas.
CARY: *Banana skins?*
MARY: Yes, a pair of slippers.

DAD: What have you got your eye on for Christmas?
DENNIS: *I've got my eye on that shiny red bike in the shop
on the high street.*
DAD: Well, you'd better keep your eye on it, because you'll
never get your bottom on it!

MAN IN SHOP: I'm trying to buy a present for my wife.
Can you help me out?
SHOP ASSISTANT: *Certainly, sir. Which way did you come
in?*

What happened when Santa's dog ate garlic?
His bark was worse than his bite!

JANE: I wish I could afford to buy a pedigree puppy for Christmas.
WAYNE: Why do you want a pedigree puppy?
JANE: Oh, I don't want one. I just wish I had enough money to buy one.

How does Santa dress in the middle of winter?
Quickly!

What do hedgehogs eat for Christmas dinner?
Prickled onions.

FARMER: The hens have been drinking the Christmas whisky.
FARMER'S WIFE: How do you know?
FARMER: They're laying Scotch eggs.

GILLY: I baked two Christmas cakes, take your pick.
BILLY: No thanks, I'll use my hammer.

Who has friends for Christmas dinner?
A cannibal.

What game do monsters play at Christmas parties?
Swallow my leader.

Where do ghosts go for a Christmas treat?
The phantomime.

What happens if you eat the Christmas decorations?
You get tinsellitis.

Christmas Things to Make and Do

Christmas Snowstorm

You will need

A screw-top jar
A small plastic toy – you could use some Christmas cake
decorations
Glycerine
Glue – not water-soluble
and the special ingredient – some glitter!

1. Fill your jar with water, and screw the lid on.
2. Now shake it about to make sure there aren't any leaks.
3. Empty the jar and re-fill it, using two parts water and
   one part glycerine. The glycerine thickens the water so
   that your glitter snow will fall slowly. Now sprinkle in
   the glitter and give it a good stir.
4. Finally, glue your toy to the bottom of the lid, and put
   the lid on tightly. Get shaking, and admire your winter
   wonderland!

Salt Dough Tree Decorations

You will need

300g plain flour
300g salt
200ml water
1 teaspoon oil
A baking tray
A selection of festive cutters

Your Christmas tree will look great, covered with these non-edible decorations.

1. Put all the ingredients into a bowl, mix them all together, then roll into a ball.
2. Roll the dough out flat. Then cut out shapes like stars and snowmen with a cutter – and make a little hole in each one so that they can be hung on the tree when they're cooked.
3. Ask an adult to pop them in the oven at 180°C / Gas Mark 4 for 20 minutes.
4. When they've cooled, you can paint them bright colours and add some sparkly string.

Wrapping Paper

print wrapping paper adds a personal touch to your
-giving – and it's lots of messy fun to make, too! You
shaped cookie cutter and a large potato, or you can
your hands into the paint and use them to make
rns.

Cut out a slice from the middle of the potato and press
the cookie cutter into it.
Then push out the shape you have cut, and dip it into
some paint – any colour you like.
3. Press the shape on to a piece of paper, and repeat to
make the coolest wrapping paper around!
4. You can also place your hands in the paint and then
press them against the paper.

Christmas

You will need

250g plain flour
125g butter
60g caster sugar

1. Mix all the ingredients together in a
    slowly knead them together to make a ball.
2. Roll out this pastry until it is about 1cm thic
    use festive cookie cutters to cut out ang
    Christmas trees and so on.
3. Place them on a greased baking tray and ask an a
    put them in the oven to cook for 10–15 minu
    160°C / Gas Mark 3.
4. Let them cool, and enjoy!

Potato
present
need a
press
patte

1.

2

Christmas Tree Paperchain

An easy-to-make decoration to take pride of place in your classroom or house.

1. Lay out two pieces of paper, and join them together with some tape.
2. Then fold the paper in half, and then back on itself again so that the paper makes a zigzag shape.
3. Draw a Christmas tree on the first face of the paper, making sure that one set of branches touches both sides of the paper. This will be the link between the sheets.
4. Then cut out the Christmas tree shape, taking care not to cut along the folds of the paper.
5. Open out the shape, and you should have a dancing string of trees – which you can decorate with different colours and glitter.

Christmas Hats

Making a festive hat is simple: take a piece of coloured paper, and roll it into a cone shape.

Secure this with tape, and then get decorating – you can use glitter, streamers and pencils and paint to make it really festive.

Gift Calendar

A perfect present for any family member – you'll need to buy a plain, tear-off calendar.

Stick this to the bottom of a sturdy piece of paper or cardboard, and decorate the background.

You could stick on a photo, or paint handprints, or write a poem and draw pictures around it.

Use some ribbon to make a loop to hang it up with.

Index of First Lines

Index of Poets

Acknowledgements

The publisher would like to thank the following for their kind permission to reprint copyright material in this book.

Bonner, Ann, 'Angels', first published in *Christmas Poems*, collected by Jill Bennett, reprinted by permission of Oxford University Press, 1999; **Fatchen, Max,** 'Beds' by permission of Johnson & Alcock Ltd; Farjeon, Eleanor: 'In the Week When Christmas Comes' and 'Christmas Stocking', first published in *Blackbird Has Spoken*, reprinted by permission of David Higham Associates; **Benson, Gerard,** 'Speeches of Kings and Shepherds', first published in *Evidence of Elephants*, Viking, 1995.

Every effort has been made to trace the copyright holders, but if any have been inadvertently overlooked then the publisher will be pleased to make the necessary arrangement at the first opportunity.